1985

Korean-American and Korean Studies
Publication Series No. 3.

TRADITIONAL THOUGHTS AND PRACTICES IN KOREA

editors
Eui-Young Yu
Earl H. Phillips

for

Association for Korean Studies in Southern California

published by

Center for Korean-American and Korean Studies
California State University, Los Angeles
Los Angeles, California

Cover Photo

In this anonymous portrait, the Neo-Confucian scholar and painter Yi Chae (1680-1746) is dressed in the informal clothing of the gentry. Yi Chae entered government service after passing the civil service examinations in 1702 and 1707. He held several high positions before retiring in 1727 to teach Confucian philosophy. His writings are still well known today. (Vertical scroll, ink and slight color on silk, 56.5 × 97.0cm, National Museum of Korea.)

ACKNOWLEDGMENTS

Among the nine essays contained in this volume six were prepared for a symposium held in Los Angeles in March 1979, sponsored by the Association for Korean Studies in Southern California. The essays by Dr. Ha Tai Kim and Dr. Byong-Kon Kim were especially written for this volume while the article "The Value System of Yi Dynasity Korea" is the work of late Dr. Hei Chu Kim. The editors are grateful to Mrs. Hei Chu Kim for her permission to publish the article.

The Center for Korean-American and Korean Studies and the editors of this volume would like to acknowledge the support and continuing encouragement they have received from the Association for Korean Studies in Southern California and from the Korean community in Los Angeles.

Los Angeles, March 1983

Authors

Yunshik Chang; Professor of Sociology, The University of British Columbia.

Griffin Dix; Ph.D., Anthropology.

Laurel Kendall; Assistant Curator, American Museum of Natural History.

Byong-Kon Kim; Professor of Music, California State University, Los Angeles.

Ha Tai Kim; Professor of Philosophy, Whittier College.

Hei Chu Kim; Formerly Associate Professor of Sociology, Western Illinois University.

Jung Young Lee; Professor of Religion, University of North Dakota.

Ellen Salem; Ph.D., History.

Barbara Young; Ph.D., Anthropology.

Editors

Earl H. Phillips; Professor of History, California State University, Los Angeles

Eui-Young Yu; Professor of Sociology, California State University, Los Angeles

Contents

Introduction

Earl H. Phillips and Eui-Young Yu

The nine essays presented in this volume represent the Humanity and Social Science disciplines, with contributions from anthropology, history, music philosophy, and sociology. Nevertheless, despite the diversity, the reader will be immediately impressed by the fact that the philosophical foundations of Korean culture and civilization are very old. And not only are they old. The underpinnings of society have shown such strength and resilience that even the casual visitor to Korea must be struck by the numerous contemporary manifestations of these ancient principles that dictate so many aspects of life, affecting everything from political organization to moral values. The essays on fortunetelling and shamanism deal with two such modern versions of old practices.

It is widely known, of course, that Confucianism and Neo-Confucianism have played a vital role for almost a thousand years in the evolution of Korean culture, and most of the essays are linked by this thread. The first, by Ha Tai Kim, examines the contributions made by the two philosophers T'oegye and Yulgok to the corpus of Neo-Confucian scholarship inherited from China. To a degree, these two sixteenth century thinkers re-stated Sung Neo-Confucianism in a Korean setting, founding their respective "Rationalist" and "Materialist" schools and giving rise to the Four Beginnings / Seven Feelings controversy. But perhaps their most important contribution was to expand on the work already commenced in Chinese Neo-Confucianism, that is, the application of a cosmological system based on the concepts of *li* and *ch'i* to nature and the human mind. Yulgok substituted T'oegye's theory of "the alternate issuance of *li* and *ch'i*" with the theory of "singular issuance of *li* and *ch'i*" and was able to lay the philosophical foundation for the examination of the workings of the mind.

Despite these Korean additions to the body of Neo-Confucianism thought, it must be remembered nevertheless that Neo-Confucianism in Korea remained firmly rooted in Chinese soil. Chu Hsi philosophy in fact became the orthodox philosophy of the Chosun (Yi) court. But despite this common heritage it is of interest to note that a very important component of Korean culture differed markedly from that of China: in Korea, the family—rather than the state—became the primary focus of loyalty. While this was less true of the *yangban* class, that class was comparatively small; as for the rest, the state (personified by the monarch) was hardly considered to be the fitting object of loyalty. The emphasis on the corporate family community—indeed, an emphasis that made the family the very cement of the national life—served to subordinate individualism to the larger good and de-emphasized individual performance.

The chapter by Hei Chu Kim deals with these and other issues while discussing the value systems that embraced Yi dynasty Korea. The author also mentions the wide range of other Confucian-derived values that played on interpersonal relations, norms, practices, and formalized etiquette that, for example, dictated the forms of speech to be used between social unequals and rigorously prescribed the public display of emotional reactions. Confucianism is also well known for the great value placed on education, but as the author points out, education remained static, mechanistic, and hidebound before the later appearance of "practical learning," revolving around memorization and the recitation of the classics. An inevitable consequence of this Confucian rigidity has been the emphasis on conformity in so many aspects of life and an intolerance of dissent. Also, a rigid hierarchical order came to prevail in all forms of social relationship.

Kim Il-bu, a nineteenth century scholar, inherited the Neo-Confucian tradition including, of course, a thorough familiarity with the Fu Hsi *Book of Change*. He was a contemporary of Chae chae-wu, the founder of Eastern Learning (*Donghak*); in fact the two men shared the same teacher, Yi Yon-dam. *Donghak* can well be viewed as a statement of nationlism, a reaction against the forces of Western cultural penetration. But Kim Il-bu was also a product of the turmoil of the nineteenth century which witnessed a people oppressed and exploited by corrupt ruling officials and a nation faced by aggressive and expansionist colonial powers. Kim Il-bu then made his own nationalist statement in his *Book of Correct Change* (1885), which can be viewed as the completion of the two earlier treatises on change. What the new work suggested, in fact, was that Korea—the contemporary prey of powerful foreign states and wracked by internal disorder, conflict, and confusion—was destined to become the very center of a new universal order, an order that would usher in peace, equality, and the harmony of all things in heaven and earth.

Jung Young Lee's article deals with this defiant statement of Korean equality, following Kim Il-bu's new arrangement of the eight trigrams and the two important transitions he made to complete the *Book of Change.*

While the *Book of Correct Change* can readily be interpreted as a manifestation of Korean nationalism, it is much more than that. Anthropologist Griffin Dix, using a "sociology of knowledge" approach in his article on folk religion, examines the concept of change in rural Korea and finds that fluctuations in personal or family fortune, while certainly attributable to random luck, are also believed to be attributable to what he calls a "folk idea of change." He argues that this is comprised of an amalgam of belief systems concerning time (the almanac) and space (geomancy), the necessary conditions being intimate contacts with the same people over long periods of time, rural immobility, and an agricultural economy.

These preconditions being met, he says, results in a shared commonality of rural experience and existence that accepts local change (say in social hierarchy) but only within the confines that it takes place within a larger perceptible—and perceived—order. Change, in fact, is order, and this overall scheme of things determines the success or failure of human events. The idea of a governing order is therefore intrinsic to the entire concept of change, and it should be pointed out that order is not only cosmological. The social world likewise requires it.

An important part of Confucian order concerned the social position of women. There is no doubt that in the previous Buddhist / Koryo period, women had been accorded—or had achieved—a considerable degree of personal freedom, but their status was challenged during the Confucian / Chosun dynasty. Ways were then sought to separate the domains of men and women by formulating codes of female conduct. The principle of *yin* and *yang,* from the *Book of Change,* was applied to human relationships, with men held to be strong and superior and women submissive and inferior. If this was achieved then the family was perfect; and if the family was perfect then society was perfect. There then commenced a complex and rigid definition of sex roles and behavior, with women consigned to be the hewers of wood and drawers of water in a male-dominated world of *yin* predominance. As Confucius himself is reported to have said to women: "At no time do you act and achieve on your own."

Yunshik Chang's essay deals with this issue of women in Confucian-based Korea, reaching the startling conclusion that women, as a survival mechanism, developed an existentialism based on the negation of existence. Equally as surprising, he suggests that women never questioned the validity of Confucian orthodoxy.

It is an accepted truism that Confucianism set the tenor of Korean life with the advent of the Yi dynasty, almost a thousand years ago, and a vast amount of scholarly work has investigated and illuminated the relationships between that philosophy and various aspects of Korean life and culture. The relationships between Confucianism and music, however, has never received the attention it deserves, which is a pity, as traditional music has been tied to Confucianism by very strong aesthetic and philosophical bonds.

Byong-kon Kim addresses these connections in his chapter on *Kagok* music, noting that there were attempts as early as the fifteenth century to purge from the repertoire music that offended Confucian standards. Such "unworthy" music should be replaced by that deemed "correct." The Master himself had suggested some guidelines of acceptability, the *Analects* recording that the music of *Ch'eng* was obscene and to be avoided while the music of *Kwan-sui* was pleasant but not obscene, mournful yet not distressing.

Intimately connected with *Kagok* music was *sijo* poetry, the essence of which, according to the *Analects,* was the avoidance of depraved thoughts. Thus, orthodoxy was established not only for the musical form but for the poetry it carried, defining the limits of development for many centuries. Nonetheless, embedded in Confucianism is the idea of orderly and ordered change, and *Kagok* music did not remain static or immutable but incorporated modifications in form and style, as well as thematic changes in the poetry. The overall goal of orthodox "correctness" remained, however.

Confucian and Neo-Confucian order in traditional Korea, both cosmological and social, was linked to the balance, symmetry, and harmony expressed in the *Book of Change*. Scholars over the centuries studied its philosophy and expounded on its wisdom in numerous interpretations and exegeses. But there is another function possible for the *Book of Change*. Knowledge of the universal scheme of things is but a short step to the possibility of predicting future developments if the book is approached in the spirit of worshipping Shang-ti, whose will can be disclosed through divination. There is thus a strong connection between the *Book of Change* and divination and the articles by Barbara Young and Laurel Kendall deal with two related although distinct aspects of contemporary divination, fortunetelling and shamanism. The number of practitioners involved attests to the strength of the spiritual tradition in modern Korea.

Professor Young writes about the *chomchaengi,* fortunetellers who ply a brisk trade divining the messages of spirits. Dr. Kendall, while dealing with contemporary shamanism, writes about a practice that predates by several centuries the appearance of Buddhism in Korea. Shamans in ancient times were the highly regarded priests of heaven worship who had the ability to communicate with the spiritual world. With Buddhism, however, the priestly function of the shamans was reduced to communication with local patron gods only, a position that was further eroded with the founding of the Yi dynasty. Confucianism then became the royal ideology, and as the new system incorporated the indigenous deities an anti-shamanistic policy began to take hold.

Although household spirits were not taken over, the "Confucianization" of life meant that men could no longer participate in the shamanistic rites of worship, with the result that women became the practitioners of essentially family cults. In this greatly reduced position, however, shamanism has enjoyed a long and strong existence, its niche in Korea's history even becoming more secure in the last generation as it has not only been studied academically but has been revived as a modern art form representing an aspect of ancient folk culture. The nation has sought to preserve such survivals. The spirited and evocative essay by Laurel Kendall certainly attests to the vitality of shamanistic practices—and spiritual belief—even in today's bustling urban environment.

The final chapter of this volume examines a Korean aspect of slavery, a theme that has had a universal history. Ellen Salem is an historian, and her essay on the slave rebellions of the Koryo period represents a model of the historian's craft. First is the description of the eight rebellions that took place in the half-century after the year 1182. But history is much more than description of past events; the historian must ask the critical question: why? In this case, why such a large number of revolts occurring in such a short space of time? The author answers the question in her analysis of the events, finding in fact that there is no single explanation. Rather, she offers a complex of reasons that flow from the general social instability of the late twelfth century, which was one of the conditions that gave rise to the new Confucian order in the succeeding dynasty.

On reaching the end of this book the reader will have become impressed by the ancient philosophical and moral foundations of Korean society. The reader with a first-hand knowledge of contemporary Korea, a country vibrant with all the dynamic forces of the twentieth century world, will also recognize the fact that these foundations have proved to be strong and tenacious. Despite the upheavals of the nineteenth and twentieth centuries, the essentials of traditional Korea still continue to flavor, dictate, and even dominate the very nature of life.

The reader, especially the one first approaching the study of Korean culture, will also have been impressed by the tremendous effect that Confucianism has had on that country. But a word of caution is in order. While the impression is correct in its generality, it is an impression that can be misleading. It is even incorrect if the view is taken that Confucianism and its manifold attributes has swept aside in the past millenium all other sources of the nation's culture history. The cultural history of a people never flows from such a single source, and in the Korean case, its cultural history is derived from a complex of sources that would have to include the physical environment of the peninsula, proximity to the rest of Asia and the oceans, Buddhism, Taoism, and a host of other material and non-material factors. Confucianism, in brief, has been important for the past nine centuries, even very important, but it has not been the only factor that has put its mark on the ever-evolving panorama of Korean culture.

With this admonition, the reader is warmly invited to partake of the following essays, designed to shed illumination on one of the world's ancient civilizations.

1 / The Difference Between T'oegye And Yulgok on the Doctrine of Li And Ch'i

HA TAI KIM

If one is asked to name two great Confucian scholars in the history of Korea, no one will dispute the mentioning of T'oegye and Yulgok. These two men are the philosophical giants in Korea who far surpass others in their depth of thought and influence upon later scholars. The fact is not to be ignored that both not only digested, interpreted and systematized Neo-Confucianism which was developed during the period of Sung, but also succeeded in the elaboration of some subtle points which were not explicitly discussed by the Sung scholars. It is due to the scholarly activities of T'oegye and Yulgok that Neo-Confucianism which flourished in China during the period of Sung was revitalized in Korea three hundred years after the death of Chu Hsi.

Although the 16th century Yi Dynasty was plagued with the invasions and threats of "Barbarians" to the north and Japanese to the south, there were numerous scholars who were dedicated to the study of Neo-Confucianism, among whom T'oegye and Yulgok are outstanding. They, together with their disciples, founded their respective schools known as "the Rationalist school" (主理派) and "the Materialist school" (主氣派), or "the Young-nam school" (嶺南學派) and "the Ki-ho school" (畿湖學派). Unfortunately, this philosophical opposition turned later into a political opposition known as "Suh-in" (西人) and "Tong-in" (東人), but it is an undeniable fact that the serious philosophical discussions between T'oegye and Yulgok, and between their disciples, deserve a recognition having its own merit.

The doctrine of *li* (理 Principle) and *ch'i* (氣 Ether of materialization) is the central theme of Neo-Confucianism, which was being discussed by all the Neo-Confucian scholars in China, but the greatest synthesizer was Chu Hsi (朱熹 1130-1200). Chu Hsi, by distinguishing between "what is above shape" (形而上) and "what is within shape" (形而下), called "instruments" (器)

for things which have shapes and forms, and *tao* (道 the way) for
the "principle" of these instruments. And he identified the *tao* of
"what is above shape" with *li* and the instruments of "what is
within shape" with *ch'i*. From this distinction, it is easy to be confused in thinking that *li* is metaphysical and *ch'i* is physical.
However, it must be noted that all the physical things can be
regarded as "instruments," because they are equipped with a
definite form, but *ch'i* is the ground and power of all things which
have shapes and forms. Therefore, *ch'i* must not be equated with
"instruments." Thus, both *li* and *ch'i* should be treated as
metaphysical concepts by which the physical universe is explained.
In Chu Hsi philosophy, *tao* is the first principle of philosophy,
known also as *T'ai-chi* (太極 Great Ultimate) and *T'ai-chi* is, in
turn, characterized by *li*. With this emphasis on *li*, Chu Hsi and
T'oegye may be grouped together as the rationalists.

Chu Hsi's rationalism has several implications. First, although
T'ai-chi cannot be described in terms of forms and shapes, basically it includes a system of *li*. Chu Hsi uses Chou Tun-yi's
(周敦頤 1017-73) expression, "Non-Ultimate is Great Ultimate,"
when he expresses the idea that *T'ai-chi* has no shapes. However,
since *T'ai-chi* is the ground of the whole universe, Chu Hsi thought
that *T'ai-chi* embraces the principles of the entire universe. Thus,
all things that exist are particular things because they have their
own principles, for without principle, it would be impossible for a
thing to exist. All existent things exist because there is a cause of existence and normative form or essence of existence, which is none
other than *li*. The totality of all principles is identified with *T'ai-chi*
by Chu Hsi, as expressed in the following words of Chu Hsi:

> Principles of all the myriad things within the universe,
> brought into one whole, constitute the Supreme Ultimate.
> The Supreme Ultimate did not originally have this name.
> It is simply an appellation applied to it.[1]

Fung Yu-lan says that *T'ai-chi* can be compared with Plato's "idea
of the Good" or Aristotle's God.[2] Here, Chu Hsi seems to suggest
Plato's "Intelligible World," and like Plato, he must be regarded
as a rationalist.

Second, Chu Hsi's rationalism implies the meaning that *li*
precedes *ch'i*. Writes he: "Thus, there is already the Principle
itself, even when its object does not yet actually exist."[3] Although

Chu Hsi advocated the priority of *li* over *ch'i,* he insisted that *li* and *ch'i* are inseparable. He feels that it is difficult to talk about which came first; but when one is forced to answer the question of origin, one can speak of the priority of *li*. It is evident that for Chu Hsi the priority of *li* is a logical one rather than a temporal one.

Third, Chu Hsi's rationalism also implies that *li* is the metaphysical reality which is a changeless, motionless and an eternal principle, a reality that is perfect without deficiency. On the other hand, *ch'i* is the motivating power of things that are subject to change, possessing movement and quiescence, capable of producing forms and shapes. Therefore, the *li* as the ultimate reality transcends forms and shapes, all limiting conditions, and furthermore, is a reality which transcends all dichotomies such as subject and object, self and the world, good and evil—dichotomies created by our reason. This reality typifies the kind of realm which Oriental philosophies often express in negative terms such as "Nothing," "Non-Ultimate," "No Mind," or "Emptiness." Says Chu Hsi, "Principle lacks volition or plan and has no creative power. Yet the fact simply is that whenever the Ether condenses into one spot, Principle is present within it."[4] One may interpret this statement as meaning that *li* as the metaphysical reality is not only indescribable in a definite manner, but also is incapable of creative function. Furthermore, Chu Hsi seems to suggest that it is only *ch'i* that is capable of having creative and conscious activities. The reason is simply that *li* has no movement and quiescence and has no creative power; therefore, it is *ch'i* rather than *li* that creates things in the universe. That is to say, *ch'i* is capable of congelation and it consolidates or dissolves into many things so as to create things in the universe. On this point, Chu Hsi simply adopts Chang Tsai's (張載 1020-77) cosmology.

Fourth, when the doctrine of *li* and *ch'i* is applied to ethics, Chu Hsi's rationalism implies that *li* is purely good while *ch'i* may yield impurity, deficiency and even evil because *ch'i* is either clear or unclear, pure or impure. To use the terminology of Western philosophy, *li* may be considered as "Being" and *ch'i* as "Nonbeing" which is sometimes regarded as the cause of evil. From this thought it is easy to see why there is a tendency among the followers of Chu Hsi to respect *li* and despise *ch'i*.

Chu Hsi recognized the two separate domains of *li* and *ch'i* in his cosmology, but it is difficult to classify him as a dualist even though he is often so classified. If one interprets his concepts of *li* and *ch'i* as two attributes of *T'ai-chi* which is one, then his position would be closer to monism, rather than dualism. At any rate, because of his identification of *T'ai-chi* with *li*, it is certain that he was a rationalist and perhaps he may even be considered as a pan-logicist like Hegel.

T'oegye (李退溪 1501-1570), who was active in Korea three hundred years after Chu Hsi, was faithful to Chu Hsi philosophy and with Yulgok was successful in establishing Chu Hsi philosophy as the official orthodox philosophy in Korea. Therefore, it must be remembered that the philosophical thinking of T'oegye and of Korean scholars after him have been more or less confined to the general framework of Chu Hsi philosophy.

The greatest concern for Korean Neo-Confucianism was how to apply the cosmology of Chinese Neo-Confucianism to the problem of psychology, so as to lay a philosophical foundation for the workings of the human mind. It is true that the Sung philosophers had already dealt with this problem, but Korean Neo-Confucianism delved into this question more deeply and penetratingly, so that it focussed its attention to what is known as the "Four-Seven Controversy," which may be considered as the most outstanding feature of Korean Neo-Confucianism. Since the cosmological doctrine of *li* and *ch'i* is always at the heart of discussion of human nature and mind, Korean Neo-Confucianism was primarily concerned with how to relate the cosmological concepts of *li* and *ch'i* to the psychological concepts of *li* and *ch'i*. The discussion of the mutual relationship between the cosmological treatment of *li* and *ch'i* and the psycholgical treatment of them has, at times, resulted in a clarification of and, at other times, caused ambiguity and confusion of the doctrine of *li* and *ch'i*.

T'oegye, following Chu Hsi philosophy, took the stance of rationalism. He reasserted Chu Hsi's rationalism by saying that "*li* is the leader of *ch'i* and *ch'i* is the follower of *li*."[5] Again, T'oegye accepted Chu Hsi's position that *li* and *ch'i* are "two yet one" and "one yet two." In reading T'oegye's writings it is difficult to determine whether he was a monist or a dualist. He simply states that *li* follows *ch'i*, yet there is no *li* without *ch'i*, and no *ch'i* without *li*. T'oegye writes:

> *Tao* is, namely, instruments and the instruments are, namely, *tao*. When we say that in the midst of emptiness and vastness myriad forms are already equipped, it does not mean that in reality *tao* is the same as instruments. When we say that things are not outside *li,* it does not mean that in reality things are the same as *li.*[6]

He believes that *li* and *ch'i* are inseparable, but *ch'i* refers to things that appear and *li* refers to the reason for such appearances. Thus, logically, we may infer that T'oegye seems to admit *T'ai-chi,* the one and the same source of both *li* and *ch'i.*

T'oegye seems to accept the position of Chu Hsi, which appears to be contradictory on the surface. This position is expressed by Chu Hsi in the following two statements: "*Li* and *ch'i* are two separate things," and "from the standpoint of things, these two can never be separated." So T'oegye recognizes that they have separate functions and also that they are inseparable in things. If one looks at this doctrine from the standpoint of Western philosophy, the best categories that would fit *li* and *ch'i* are Aristotle's concepts of form and matter. It is comparable to the view that form and matter are not the same thing, but not a thing that exists in the phenomenal world is without the combination of form and matter. Therefore, while the form and the matter of a particular thing assume a particular determination, the Neo-Confucian *li* and *ch'i* as the creative principles of the universe are without any determination. Hence, both of them must be regarded as formal concepts comparable to Aristotle's "pure form" and "pure matter." From this consideration, I would regard not only *li,* but also *ch'i* is as logical postulates, contrary to Fung Yu-lan's opinion that *ch'i* is a positive concept when he says: "In Chang Tsai's and the Cheng-Chu system alike, the concept of *ch'i* is not a formal concept, but a positive one."[7]

One problem that arises from T'oegye's attempt to apply the cosmological concepts of *li* and *ch'i* to psychology is his insistence that the "Four Beginnings" (四端) are issued from *li* (理發) and the "Seven Feelings" (七情) are issued from *ch'i* (氣發). A clarification in the use of these terms is in order. The meaning of *li* and *ch'i* as used in cosmology is not the same as the meaning of these terms as used in psychology, and that these two meanings must be distinguished. Cosmologically, the concepts of *li* and *ch'i* have the meaning of "form" and "matter" as stated above, but psychologically, they stand for "reason" and "senses."

Before discussing T'oegye's philosophy, it will be necessary to explain first the meaning of "the Four Beginnings," and "the Seven Feelings." The phrase "Four Beginnings" is derived from Mencius' writings. According to Mencius, human nature possesses four virtues, namely: *Jen* (仁 Human-heartedness), *I* (義 Righteousness), *Li* (禮 Propriety) and *Chih* (智 Wisdom); consequently, human nature is basically and inherently good. There are four feelings that arise in the mind, namely the feeling of commiseration (*ts'e yin* 惻隱), the feeling of shame and dislike (*hsiu wu* 羞惡), the feeling of modesty and of yielding (*tz'u jang* 辭讓), the sense of right and wrong (*shih fei* 是非). These feelings are regarded as the beginnings of *Jen, I , Li* and *Chih* respectively. Thus, these four feelings are called "the Four Beginnings."

The phrase "Seven Feelings," which is found in *Li Chi* (Book of Rites), refers to emotion arising in the mind when the mind is in contact with the external world through the senses. These seven feelings are joy, anger, pity, fear, love, hate and desire.

T'oegye was prompted to give serious thought to the question of *li* and *ch'i* in conjunction with human nature by reading the statement, "Four Beginnings issue at *li* and Seven Feelings issue at *ch'i,"* in "Diagram of the Decree of Heaven" drawn by Chung Chu-man (鄭秋巒 1509-1561).[8] T'oegye, noting Chu Hsi's remark that "Four Beginnings are *li's* issuance and Seven Feelings are *ch'i's* issuance,"[9] concluded that Four Beginnings are "*li*-issuance" (理發) and Seven Feelings are "*ch'i*-issuance" (氣發). The difference between T'oegye and Yulgok is dependent upon how one interprets the original meaning of the above statement made by Chu Hsi. Yulgok points out that while Chu Hsi's original statement was intended to be a general statement, the later philosophers made a sharp distinction between *li* and *ch'i.* Yulgok insists that Chu Hsi's statement should be interpreted as meaning that Four Beginnings are spoken of only *li* and Seven Feelings are spoken of both *li* and *ch'i,* and not to be taken as meaning that Four Beginnings have "*li*-issuance" first, and Seven Feelings have "*chi*-issuance" first.[10]

Why did T'oegye insist upon the theory of "*li*-issuance"? One reason is that T'oegye saw the role of *li* and *ch'i* from a psychological and ethical point of view, rather than a cosmological point of view.[11] Another reason is that T'oegye wanted to emphasize Mencius' theory that human nature is basically good.

Two comments on T'oegye's theory of "*li*-issuance" must be made. First, T'oegye's theory of "*li-issuance*" and "*ch'i*-issuance" would become intelligible if *li* is interpreted as "reason" and *ch'i* as "senses." The mind may be said to respond to stimuli from the external world and the responses of the mind take the form of cognition and feeling. Here "Four Beginnings" and "Seven Feelings" are all but feelings, and T'oegye himself admits this. But there is also a volitional aspect in the mind. When an action is about to take place, the question concerning motivation may be posed: is it from reason or from senses (selfish desire)? Plato, viewing the soul being composed of three parts — rational, passionate and appetitive — believed that if one's action is motivated by rational principles, one possesses a healthy and just soul. Thus, if one interprets T'oegye's theory of "*li*-issuance" as rationally motivated action, his theory becomes understandable.

Second, if human nature is *li* which is purely good, as the Neo-Confucian scholars hold, then the question is why the need to talk about "issuance" at all? The Neo-Confucian scholars often use expressions such as "*wei-fa*" (未發 not yet issued, imminent issuance) and "*i-fa*" (已發 already issued, accomplished issuance). "*Wei-fa*" refers to the original nature of man which is identified with *li* and this is called "*tao-hsin*" (道心 the mind of *tao*). Therefore, if one understands the word "*fa*" (issuance) as meaning the movement of the mind as triggered by the mind's contact with the external world, then what is issuing is certainly the mind, not *li* itself.

Third, T'oegye seems to deviate from the cosmology of Sung scholars when his theory of "Four-Seven" is examined. The concept of *li* employed in the theory of human nature and mind by T'oegye is not only different from, but contradicts the concept of *li* articulated by Sung philosophers. In defining *li*, Chu Hsi said:

> It is the Ether that has the capacity to condense and thus create, whereas Principle lacks volition or plan and has no creative power . . . . Principle constitutes only a pure, empty, and vast world, utterly shapeless and hence incapable of producing anything, whereas the Ether has the capacity to ferment and condense and in this way bring things into being.[12]

Following his predecessors, Chu Hsi insists that there is no move-

ment and quiescence in *li*. This thought clearly shows that *li* is the
Great Ultimate and also *tao*. The *tao,* as suggested by Lao-tzu, is
the ultimate reality which is un-nameable and indescribable. This
reminds one of the Oriental Nothingness which transcends all
language. Therefore, *li* as the ultimate reality transcends thought
and feelings and all opposite concepts created by thought, such as
movement and quiescence, good and evil, affirmation and negation. In this sense, *li* in Neo-Confucian philosophy may be likened
to "Brahman" in Hindu philosophy and *Sunyata* (void) in Buddhist philosophy.

In spite of this, T'oegye in his theory of human nature and
mind asserts that there is movement and quiescence in *li*. Thus,
T'oegye is sharply in disagreement with the theory of *li* as discussed
in the cosmology of Sung Neo-Confucianism. T'oegye himself
seems to have caught this contradiction, for he developed a
modified view by dividing *li* into two parts: *li* as substance (*t'i* 体)
and *li* as function (*yung* 用). By dividing *li* into two parts, he held
the view that the non-creative power is *li's* substance and the
creative power is *li's* function. He writes: "The original substance
of *li* lacks volition or plan and has no creative power, but we
discover it everywhere due to the subtle function of *li*."[13] Since the
function of *li* is believed to be found only in the mind, T'oegye's
statement ultimately supports his theory of "*li*-issuance."

Unlike the Sung philosophers, T'oegye, in order to make his
theory of "*li*-issuance" consistent, persistently held the view that
there is movement and quiescence in *li*. He writes:

> When *li* moves, *ch'i* is subsequently generated, and when *ch'i* moves, *li* subse-
> quently emerges. When Chou Tun-i said that *yang* or light is born by the
> movement of *T'ai-chi,* he meant that *ch'i* is created by the movement of *li*.
> Chou I also speaks of seeing the mind of heaven and earth, which means that
> *li* emerges from the movement of *ch'i*."[14]

However, this writer's interpretation of Chou Tun-i's statement is that there are two aspects in *T'ai-chi, li* and *ch'i,* and that it
is through the activity of *ch'i,* not of *li,* that *yang* is born.

The main reason why T'oegye recognized movement in *li* can
be attributed to his view that *li* as the ultimate reality is not dead,
but alive. T'oegye maintains that if one admits only of the "non-
action" of the substance of *li* and ignore the subtle function of *li,*
then *li* would be treated as a dead thing. He goes on to say that to

treat *li* as a dead thing is an admission that we do not understand the real meaning of the *tao*.[15]

Here again, T'oegye seems to part ways from the concept of *li* as defined by the Sung scholars. The very meaning of *li* as the ultimate reality, if one accepts the basic assumption, should not only transcend thoughts, feelings and volition, but also the dichotomy of life and death. Despite his faithfulness in following Chu Hsi, why did T'oegye deviate from the Sung scholars on the concept of *li*? Certainly, it cannot be surmised that T'oegye was unaware of this deviation. But if he did deviate consciously and deliberately from the Sung philosophers, there must be sufficient reason for doing so. The probable reason for this may be that T'oegye was strongly opposed to Buddhism and Taoism. Therefore, it is safe to assume that T'oegye wanted to reestablish the position of classical Confucianism against the theory of the Sung scholars, the theory which was transformed under the influence of Buddhism and Taoism.

T'oegye expands his theory of "Four-Seven" to the field of Ethics in the following statement:

> The issuance of Four Beginnings is purely from *li*; therefore, no evil can be found in them. The issuance of Seven Feelings, however, includes *ch'i;* therefore, both good and evil can be found in them.[16]

As a result of criticisms directed at him by Ki Ko-bong (奇高峯 1527-1572), one of his able disciples, T'oegye was forced to modify his position and arrived at his final position which reads: "Speaking of Four, *li* issues and *ch'i* follows them. Speaking of Seven, *ch'i* issues and *li* rides them."[17]

Like Chu Hsi, T'oegye recognizes the dual function of *li* and *ch'i* and because of it, he believed that it was possible to have both issuances; hence, he held that "*li*-issuance" brings Four Beginnings and that "*ch'i*-issuance" brings Seven Feelings. At the same time, again like Chu Hsi, recognizing the inseparability of *li* and *ch'i*, he concluded: "Speaking of Four, *li* issues and *ch'i* follows them. Speaking of Seven, *ch'i* issues and *li* rides them."

Furthermore, T'oegye, by making a sharp distinction between *tao-hsin* (道心) and *jen-hsin* (人心), saw that *tao-hsin* consists of Four Beginnings which come from "*li*-issuance," and therefore, it is purely good, while *jen-hsin* consists of Seven Feelings which come from "*ch'i*-issuance," and therefore, it can be both good and bad. He went one step further by identifying *tao-hsin* with Four Beginnings, and *jen-hsin* with Seven Feelings (人心 七情是也 道心 四端是也).[18]

The "Four-Seven controversy" which was debated in the correspondence between T'oegye and Ki Ko-bong reveals that Ki Ko-bong's position was really a stepping stone to Yulgok's philosophy. Ki Ko-bong, emphasizing Chu Hsi's idea that *li* and *ch'i* are inseparable, came to hold a theory of "the simultaneous issuance of *li* and *ch'i*" (理氣共發一途說). He pointed out that Seven Feelings are all the feelings that there are, and Four Beginnings merely refer to those of the Seven which are only good. He also introduced the idea that Seven Feelings actually contain Four Beginnings. Thus, it is easy to detect in the thought of Ki Ko-bong ideas that are to be developed in Yulgok's philosophy.

Yulgok 李栗谷 1536-1584), who was thirty years younger than T'oegye, earnestly and enthusiastically participated in the debate of Korean Neo-Confucianism and presented a system of his own, but it must be borne in mind that he followed essentially the line of arguments which T'oegye had initiated and that he never stepped out of the general framework of Chu Hsi philosophy. Following Chu Hsi and T'oegye, he maintained that *li* is the lord of *ch'i* and *ch'i* is the instrument of *li*. It is in his discussion of human nature and mind that he gave his original view, which is to be distinguished from T'oegye. Yulgok seems to be more consistent in his treatment of the concepts of *li* and *ch'i* in his cosmology and psychology, and in the end, he is more faithful to the ideas suggested by the Sung philosophers, while T'oegye seems to transcend or ignore the Buddhistic and Taoistic influences contained in the ideas of the Sung philosophers.

T'oegye made a distinction between *tao-hsin* and *jen-hsin,* identifying the mind of Four Beginnings with *tao-hsin* and the mind of Seven Feelings with *jen-hsin,* and also separated feelings into two groups: those of "*li*-issuance" and those of "*ch'i*-issuance." In opposition to this, Yulgok held the view that there is only one mind and one feeling, and he pointed out that T'oegye's theory of "*li*-issuance" was superfluous, for all feelings are issued from *ch'i* alone.

His view is made clear in the following quotations from his writings:

There is only one mind, but the reason for speaking of *tao-hsin* and *jen-hsin* is because we are making the distinction between the heaven-conferred nature, and forms and Ether. There is also one feeling, but the reason for speaking of Four and Seven is because we are differentiating the time when we speak only of *li* from the time when we speak of both *li* and *ch'i*. Therefore, although *tao-hsin* and *jen-hsin* cannot be combined together, one can come before the other. Although Four Beginnings cannot embrace Seven Feelings, Seven Feelings include Four Beginnings. I, therefore, wish to say that Seven Feelings are more complete than Four Beginnings and that Four Beginnings are purer than Seven Feelings.[19]

He goes on to say:

Even though our mind is now channelled through the rightness of the heavenly-conferred nature, if we mix with private desires and fail to realize the good, we start out with *tao-hsin* but end up with *jen-hsin*. On the contrary, although our mind is initially stirred by shapes and Ether, if it does not violate the right principles, it is no different from *tao-hsin*. Again, although the mind initially violates the right principles, if it, becoming aware of its wrongs, does not follow desires, then it starts out with *jen-hsin,* but ends up with *tao-hsin*. The reason for this is that *tao-hsin* and *jen-hsin* are not confined to the realm of feelings, but associated with both feelings and volition.[20]

In an attempt to give a unifying principle for *tao-hsin* and *jen-hsin,* and for Four Beginnings and Seven Feelings which T'oegye had distinguished, Yulgok provides a coherent theory of the mind as follows:

We must realize the fact that the nature, the mind, the feelings, and the will are all related to each other, yet having different territories. How are they related to each other? The *wei-fa* (not yet issued) of the mind is nature and its *i-fa* (already issued) is feelings. After the issuance of feelings, the will measures them. Why do they have different territories? It is the realm of the nature when the mind is in quiescence and calmness; it is the realm of the feelings when the mind is moving through the contact with the external world; it is the realm of the will when the mind compares and measures the things being sensed. Thus the mind is one but has several territories.[21]

For Yulgok, as it was with Chu Hsi, the underlying principle beneath human mind is *li* which is identified with the original nature of man. However, Yulgok believed that there is nothing else but seven feelings which constitute the totality of the mind's function and that these feelings are issued from *ch'i*. Thus, rejecting T'oegye's theory of "*li*-issuance," Yulgok recognized only "*ch'i*-issuance." From T'oegye's statement, "*li* issues and *ch'i* follows them, and *ch'i* issues and *li* rides them," Yulgok found only the second clause to be valid. Thus Yulgok substituted T'oegye's theory of "the alternate issuance of *li* and *ch'i*" (理氣互發説) by the theory of "singular issuance of *li* and *ch'i* (理氣一途説).

If Yulgok's theory of "Four-Seven" is examined more it is found that he agrees basically with Ki Ko-bong on the view that Seven Feelings are the totality of mind's function and Four Beginnings are none other than feelings that are good among seven feelings. On this point he has the following to say:

> Four Beginnings are nothing but the good feelings among Seven Feelings. Seven Feelings are the totality of feelings which include Four Beginnings . . . Therefore, Four Beginnings are but another name for good feelings, and when we speak of Seven Feelings, Four Beginnings are already contained in them.[22]

With this idea in mind, Yulgok attempted to distribute Four Beginnings and Seven Feelings, a task which is regarded as difficult even by Chu Hsi.

Yulgok classified the Seven Feelings in such a way that Four Beginnings are actually included in them. This classification may be illustrated thus.[23]

I. Feelings of joy, pity, love and desire	Be joyful when there is something to be joyful about. Be sorrowful in mourning. Love the endeared persons. When you see truth, try to seek it; when you see a sage, try to imitate him.	The Beginning of *jen*
II. Feeling of anger, hate	Be indignant when necessary. Hate one who deserves to be hated.	The Beginning of *I*
III. Feeling of fear	Be fearful before a respected and noble person.	The Beginning of *Li*
IV. To know what is proper for one to do when joy, anger, pity and fear are aroused		The Beginning of *Chih*

Again, he distributed Four Beginnings to Seven Feelings as follows:

> *Ts'e yin* (Beginning) belongs to love (Feeling); *hsiu wu* (Beginning) belongs to hate (Feeling); *tz'u jang* (Beginning) belongs to fear (Feeling); *shi fei* (Beginning) is a feeling to know the legitimacy and illegitimacy of joy and anger. Thus Four Beginnings have no separate existence other than Seven Feelings. Therefore, Four Beginnings are an expression pertaining to *tao-hsin,* whereas

Seven Feelings are an expression pertaining to both *tao-hsin* and *jen-hsin*, and it is wrong to speak of *tao-hsin* and *jen-hsin* as if they are completely separated.[24]

In his discussion of *li* and *ch'i*, Yulgok introduced a theory which is called "the subtlety of *li* and *ch'i* (理氣之妙), a theory synthesizing the two views of *li* and *ch'i* which were held by Chu Hsi. The two views are: (2) *li* and *ch'i* are two different things; (2) they are inseparable. With his theory of "the subtlety of *li* and *ch'i*," Yulgok rejects T'oegye's emphasis on the view that *li* and *ch'i* are two different things, the view which resulted in him proposing the separate functions of *li* and *ch'i* in terms of "*li*-issuance" and "*ch'i*-issuance."

It seems that with this theory Yulgok intends to show that the origin and source of *li* and *ch'i* are the same, as the following statement clearly shows:

The theory of 'the subtlety of *li* and *ch'i*' is a difficult view to understand. The source of *li* is only one and the source of *ch'i* is also only one . . . *Ch'i* does not depart from *li* and *li* does not leave *ch'i* either. Therefore, we may conclude that *li* and *ch'i* are one.[25]

Yulgok's theory can be understood if his statement is interpreted as meaning that there is one *T'ai-chi* and it has two attributes, namely *li* and *ch'i*.

The reason why Yulgok is labelled as a materialist or etherist is because he insisted that all things including man and nature are derived by the movement of *ch'i*. On this point, he agrees with Chang Tsai in China and Suh Wha-tam in Korea. They believed that *ch'i* is the material cause for creation or evolution, but they have never denied the role of *li* in the process of nature.

If an attempt is made to reconstruct the relationship of *li* and *ch'i* in Neo-Confucianism, it may be said that *T'ai-chi* is the ultimate reality and the way of *T'ai-chi* is called *tao*. *T'ai-chi* is what Western philosophers call "Being," which is one. Thus, *T'ai-chi* is a monistic reality. There are two attributes of *T'ai-chi*: namely, *li* and *ch'i*. *Ch'i* is the motivating power of generations of things and the material cause of things, and *li* is the reason and principle of all things that exist. Therefore, *li* and *ch'i* cannot be separated when anything that is determined and existent is considered; for if a thing must exist, it must combine *li* and *ch'i*.

If one looks into Yulgok's philosophy from the standpoint just described, his philosophy seems to say that all things issued are of *ch'i* and the reason for issuance is *li*. Without *ch'i*, there will be no issuance; without *li*, there is no reason for issuance. Thus, it seems that Yulgok is more logically consistent with the Sung scholars than T'oegye. His harmony with the theory of Sung philosophy can be easily detected from the following two statements of Yulgok:

> *Li* is above shape and *ch'i* is within shape. These two cannot be separated from one another. Therefore, the issuance and function of them is one and the same.[26]

> *Li* has no shape but *ch'i* has shape. *Li* has no action but *ch'i* has action. *Li* with no shape and non-action becomes the master of that which has shape and action. *Ch'i* is that which has shape and action and an instrument of that which has no shape and non-action. Since *li* has no shape while *ch'i* has shape, there is "the pervasiveness of *li* and the confinement of *ch'i*" (理通氣局). Since *li* has no action and *ch'i* has action, *ch'i* issues and *li* rides them. What is the meaning of the pervasiveness of *li*? *Li* has no beginning and no end, no priority and no posteriority. Therefore, we cannot speak of before and after with the issuance of *li*.[27]

It is evident that here the concept of non-shape and non-action of *li* was inherited from Sung Neo-Confucian thought. The idea that *li* is non-action is equated with Chu Hsi's concept of the non-creativity of *li*. Thus, Yulgok rejected T'oegye's theory of "*li*-issuance" by pointing out that this theory involves a contradiction for *li* is non-active and non-creative.

In conclusion, Yulgok consistently applied the theory of *li* and *ch'i* as formulated in the cosmology of Sung Neo-Confucianism to his theory of nature and mind. Thus, he was able to present a theory which is harmonious between cosmology and psychology. In fact, he sees that the workings of Heaven and Earth are similar with those of the mind.

Says he:

> The events of Heaven and Earth are parallel to the function of the mind. It is possible to talk about '*li*-issuance' and '*ch'i*-issuance' if there is a division between the changes of *li* and the changes of *ch'i* in Heaven and Earth. How is it possible for us to talk about '*Li*-issuance and '*ch'i*-issuance' while there is no distinction between the changes of *li* and *ch'i*? If our mind is different from the natural changes in the universe, it is beyond my comprehension.[28]

In his letter to Sung Wu-kei (成牛溪 1535-1598), Yulgok writes: "According to Chu Hsi, the mind's perception is only one, but some originate from the rightness of the heaven-conferred nature, and others originate from the privacy of shape and ether. Since he placed the letter of *hsin* (ᛁᏓ) before, the mind is *ch'i.*"[29] This statement implies that all the functions of the mind are due to *ch'i*. Therefore, it is understandable that the followers of T'oegye who held the theory of "*li*-issuance" called Yulgok's philosophy materialism or etherialism. However, it must be pointed out that Yulgok was no less a rationalist than Chu Hsi and T'oegye. He never denies the role of *li* in the process of nature. His discussion was primarily focussed on the issuance of things in the world, the things with form and shape, and he firmly believed that these things are issued from *ch'i*, not from *li*. Yet his insistence on this point does not entail the rejection of *li* as the principle of the world and the reason for the existence of things.

Notes

1. Quoted in Fung Yu-lan's *A History of Chinese Philosophy* (Princeton, N.J.: Princeton University Press, 1953), II: 537.
2. See *ibid.,* p. 537.
3. Quoted in Fung, *History,* II: 536.
4. Quoted in Fung, *History,* II: 542.
5. *T'oegye Jun-suh* (The Complete Works of T'oegye) (Seoul: Daedong Munwha Research Center, Sungkyunkwan University, 1959), II: 141.
6. *Ibid.,* I:430.
7. Fung Yu-lan, *The Spirit of Chinese Philosophy* (Boston: Beacon Press, 1962), p. 190.
8. Pae Chong-ho, *Hanguk Yu Hak Sa* (History of Korean Confucianism) (Seoul: Yonsei University Press, 1974), p. 72.
9. *Chu-tzu Yu-lei,* ch. 53.
10. *Yulgok Jun-suh Chung Sun* (Selections from Yulgok's Complete Works) (Seoul: Yulgok Sunsang Kinyum Sa-up Hoe, 1951), pp. 135, 144.
11. Professor Park Chong-hong in his *Hanguk Sasangsa Longo* (Essays on the History of Korean Thought) (Seoul: Suhmun Dang, 1977) makes the following statement which supports this point: "The characteristic of T'oegye's philosophy in the pursuit of *li,* is that he liked *Hsin Ching* (the Book of the Mind) so much that he attempted to look upon *li* primarily from the standpoint of the study of the mind." (p. 100).
12. Quoted in Fung, *History,* II: 543.
13. *T'oegye Jun-suh,* I: 465.
14. *Ibid.,* I: 608.
15. See *T'oegye Jun-suh,* I: 465.
16. *Ibid.,* I: 402.
17. *Ibid.,* I: 417.
18. *Ibid.,* I: 818.

19. *Yulgok Jun-suh Chung Sun,* p. 133.
20. *Ibid.,* p. 134.
21. *Ibid.,* pp. 192-3.
22. *Ibid.,* pp. 633-4.
23. See *ibid.,* p. 146.
24. *Ibid.,* p. 147.
25. *Ibid.,* p. 158.
26. *Ibid.,* p. 150.
27. *Ibid.,* p. 644.
28. *Ibid.,* p. 144.
29. *Ibid.,* p. 169.

Bibliography

Chang, Carsun. *The Development of Neo-Confucian Thought.* New York, Bookman Associates, 1957.

De Bary, Wm Theo. *The Unfolding of neo-Confucianism.* New York, Columbia University Press, 1975.

Fung, Yu-lan. *A History of Chinese Philosophy.* 2 volumes. Princeton, N.J. Princeton University Press, 1952, 1953.

Fung Yu-lan. *The Spirit of Chinese Philosophy.* Boston, Beacon Press, 1962.

Metzger, Thomas A. *Escape From Predicament, neo-Confucianism and China's Evolving Political Culture.* New York, Columbia University Press, 1977.

Nivison and Wright. *Confucianism in Action.* Stanford, Stanford Univeristy Press, 1959.

T'oegye Jun-suh (The Complete Works of T'oegye). Seoul, Daedong Cultural Research Center, Sungkyunkwan University, 1959, 2 volumes.

Yulgok Jun-suh Chung Sun (Selections from Yulgok's Complete Works). Seoul, Yulgok Sunsang Kinyum Sa-up Hoe, 1951.

Chang chi-yun. *Chosun Yuhak Yunwon* (The Origins of Korean Confucianism). I, Seoul, Samsung Munwha Library, 1975.

Kim Kyung-chuk. *Yulgok Eh Yunkyu* (Studies in Yulgok). Seoul, Hanguk Yunkyu Tosuhkwan, 1960.

Lee Byung-do. *Yulgok Eh Sangai wa Sasang* (The Life and Thought of Yulgok). Seoul, Suhmun Dang, 1973.

Lee Chun-ho. *Yulgok Eh Sasang* (The Thought of Yulgok). Seoul, Hyun-am Sa, 1973.

Pae Chong-ho. *Hanguk Yu Hak Sa* (History of Korean Confucianism). Seoul, Yonsei University Press, 1974.

Park Chong-hong. *Hanguk Sasangsa Longo* (Essays on the History of Korean Thought). Seoul, Suhmun Dang, 1977.

Shin Il-chul. *Hanguk Sasang-ga sip-i-in* (Twelve Korean Thinkers). Seoul, Hyun-am Sa, 1975.

Chosun Eh Yu Hak Ja Pal-in (Eight Confucian Scholars in Chosun). Seoul, Shinkyu Munwha Sa, 1974.

2 / The Value System of Yi Dynasty Korea

The value system of a society is the set of widely held normative judgments that define the "good" society. As this set of values is shared by most members of that society it may be referred to as the value system of the society. This, however, is only an ideal-typical definition of value system; for, in reality, there would be more than one set of values in a given society. This is true because not all members of a society would share the same set of values at the requisite level. The above statement implies that in every given society there would be a hierarchy of values that is arranged according to the relative priority the members assign to various sets of values.

This paper is concerned with locating the value system of Yi Korea with a view to delimiting and arranging different sets of values in a hierarchical order. This analytical scheme would elicit the primary central values and all the other secondary values of the society.

Of the broad categories of values underlying the four system problems,[1] the highest priority was assigned to the integrative value in Yi dynasty. In such a society, social action is largely governed by the value standards of "particularism" and "quality;" that is, social action has significance only for a particular actor in particular relations with particular objects and more emphasis is placed on the actor's ascriptive attributes than on his performance. A society with such a set of value standards tends to be concerned more with social integration, that is, the maintenance of the existing system, than with goal attainment or adaptation to the environment. This implies that all societies have all of the above concerns in one degree or another and concomitant value standards, but not all societies assign primacy to the same concern, be it integration, adaptation, or goal attainment. The integrative value is in turn expressed through the values of solidarity and harmony within a given collectivity such as family, village, or the nation.

In the Yi dynasty the value standards underlying social action tended to be particularisitic, emphasizing commitment to the collectivities to which one belonged, without due regard to commitment to universal values such as truth or justice. In Tokugawa Japan, too, the particularistic commitment prevailed extensively but it was extended all the way to the state.[2] This tendency is evinced by the strong loyalty to the symbol of the state, the emperor. In contrast, in Yi Korea the primary object of loyalty hardly extended beyond the boundary of family whose head monopolized the loyalties of its members. To be sure, the concepts of loyalty (忠) and filial piety (孝) are equally found in the Yi Korean value system—the concepts based on the five cardinal relationships of Confucius. But the concept of loyalty was not widely diffused among the general public but confined to a small group of *yangbans* in power. For the rest of the population, the state and its symbol, the king and his officialdom, were not regarded as fitting object of loyalty. Thus, the object of loyalty was directed to the smaller collectivity and its symbol, the family head.

To promote integration means to confront and solve the specific coordinative problems that arise when the units of a system mutually interfere with each other. Successful solution of coordinative problems would lead to harmony in the collectivity. The way in which Yi Korea promoted harmony is illustrated by the well-integrated set of attitudes and values for promoting good relations at the expense of justice and truth. Whenever any serious conflict developed, recourse was to the saving of the "faces" of the individuals involved, their families and the community, rather than to the universalistic moral standards. Any antisocial behavior of an individual was apt to be regarded as a temporary lapse rather than an indication of moral decay, and everyone was eager to make allowance for the person responsible and encouraged him to resume normal behavior. It was, in other words, far more important to maintain good social relations than to insist on some abstract principles with which they were not familiar.

Maintenance of harmony requires the minimization of potential conflicts and frictions. As a social mechanism controlling potential conflicts and frictions, Yi Korea elaborately formalized interpersonal relationships. Again, Confucian formalism played a vital role in this connection. The concept of *li* (禮), or propriety, one of the cardinal virtues in Confucianism, was one of the natural consequences of the strict distinctions of social ranks, for it proved efficient in maintaining the order of Yi society. It is inevitable that the concept of *li* resulted in formalism in interpersonal relationships, for the concept originally came from rituals. The parallel to the close relation between class system, *li,* and formalism can be seen in any military organization in which well-defined sets of prerogatives, duties and responsibilities are differentially assigned and formalized behavioral patterns are specified according to different ranks. The elaborately graded forms of Korean language illustrate this formalism; a clearly defined form of speech was to be used in relation to one's social superiors, another form to equals, and still another form to inferiors.

With respect to the adaptive values, characterized by the combination of the universalistic and performance value standards, any adaptive behavior in Yi Korea was discouraged by the primary emphasis placed on the integrative values. It was the welfare and harmony of a narrowly defined collectivity, be it family, village or social class, that was given the primacy over the individual's welfare. The rigidly circumscribed structures of family, community and social stratification illustrate the secondary value accorded to the adaptive values in Yi Korea. The family's corporate aspects of sharing and pooling of resources, the joint contribution of effort by the members, and the control of property by the family head continuously subordinated individual desires and interests to those of the family and lineage. This economic dependence as well as the socio-psychological dependence, which derived from the former, frustrated and discouraged any potential creativeness, initiative, or competitive efforts by the individual. Such individual efforts were regarded as detrimental to the achievement of harmony of the collectivity. The adaptive behavior was further inhibited by the lack of the performance emphasis evidenced by the attitude toward work. Since the individual was completely dependent upon his family and lineage, both economically and socio-psychologically, he was not given any incentives to engage in work as diligently as he could. Work, therefore, was basically a necessary evil, performance of which did not have any direct relevance to one's own interests and desires. A keen foreign observer diagnosed the attitude toward work among the Koreans near the end of the Yi dynasty:

They lack the energy and ambition of the Japanese, the thrift, industry and strength of the Chinese. Indolence is a national character. The Korean is content to take life as easily as possible. He is never so happy as when he is supported by some wealthy relation or has some government office which relieves him from the necessity of labor.[3]

The fact that the military, an adaptive arm of the polity, had to yield precedence to its counterparts of equal rank in the civil branch further reinforces the above assertion about the Yi Korean value system relative to the adaptive values.[4]

Political values were rather weak compared to those of Tokugawa Japan and Ching China. In Yi Korea the particularistic tie to one's collectivity in the form of loyalty was superseded by one's tie to the non-state collectivity, the family, in the form of filial piety. Loyalty was valued only when it had some instrumental values in maintaining the solidarity of the family. The rather weak political values are connected with the lack of the value standard of performance. As noted previously, the ascriptive, rather than performance, value standard permeated all aspects of the social structure of Yi Korea, whether it was social class, the family, or the government bureaucracy.

In contrast, the politics of Tokugawa Japan and Ching China were characterized by relatively strong value standards of performance. In Ching China the top status elements under the emperor were structured in achievement terms through the open examination system. This performance-oriented system allowed some degree of social mobility and promoted motivation for personal performance and achievement. The emphasis on performance in Tokugawa Japan can be seen in the sharp differentiation between status and role, implying that status did not carry prestige and power automatically, without the consideration of the actual role performance.

The combination of limited particularism and the lack of performance values seemed to have had an important implication for the problem of legitimating those in power outside the kinship unit. Within the kinship unit, the head of household had very real authority over all activities of the members. Since the familial authority was determined by ascriptive criteria such as age, sex, and generation, legitimating the authority of a leader outside the kinship unit was almost impossible. Thus, although a man would accept the authority of his father, older brother or uncle, he would not recognize anyone else's efforts to control and influence his activities. In the case of Tokugawa Japan, the value standard of particularism in the form of loyalty to one's collectivity was more generalized to the extent that it was primarily directed to the larger collectivity and its head, the emperor. This generalized particularism in the sphere of polity served as "a functional equivalent to universalism in the process of the rationalization and extension of power."[5]

The relatively weak position of the Yi government clearly illustrates the general weakness of political values. Occasionally, however, Yi Korea shifted its primary emphasis to political values, largely in emergency conditions where the goal of protecting the system from disruption became urgent.

Cultural values, which serve as the motivating force for maintaining general patterns of normative order, were rather strong in Yi Korea but subordinated to the integrative values. The strong values were inculcated in the individuals for the sole purpose of maintaining the status quo through various mechanisms. For the purpose of this analysis, two clusters of cultural values will be distinguished; a cluster of educational-religious values and another of expressive values.

The interrelationship of educational and religious values was necessarily close in Yi Korea since a considerable part of the content of the educational pattern was the inculcation of the religious pattern. The content of education and learning in particular consisted largely of inculcation of metaphysics and social etiquettes of Confucianism. Confucian teachings were regarded as the only and the highest "truth." The educational pursuit of any thing other than Confucian teachings was discouraged as unfit for a cultivated man. The learning process involved the mechanistic memorization and transcription of Confucian classics without emphasizing the need for individual thinking and judgment. The Confucian learned man was highly adept at reciting and writing classics but lacked theoretical and scientific thinking. The knowledge of Confucian classics was valued for itself rather than for its theoretical or practical utility. An inevitable consequence of this particularistic orientation to truth was the high degree of intolerance of dissident views. Debate (where the free exchange of ideas and opinions is used as a means to arrive at truth) was impossible among academic circles, since dogmatism and high-handed authority had the upper-hand over truth.

In the latter half of the Yi dynasty, however, there emerged a group of Confucian scholars who rejected the formalistic Confucian education and advocated the need for practical sciences. This group called *Silhak-pa* (實學派), or the school of practical learning, headed by scholars like Yi lk and Chong Yak-yong, could not override the mainstream of cultural values. Be that as it may, the value of learning was strong. The importance ascribed to the relationship between a student and his teacher indicated the strong value of learning. The teacher was only next to parents in importance, and even the teacher's wife carried the appellation of "teacher-mother" in whom a student might confide his personal problems.

The expressive values refer to the values that channel such emotional reactions as anger, grief, pleasure and love into particular areas acceptable to the society. All societies must have some institutionalized mode and degree of expression of such emotions since the unrestricted display of any of the emotions might lead to the disruption of society.

In Yi Korea, the display of emotional reaction was strongly inhibited; high value was placed on composure and self-control. The inhibition of emotional display was accompanied by a highly institionalized standard for the display of emotion. At the death of a family member, a given type of weeping was called for, but its expression was limited in both time and place. Outside the designated time and place a person's grief was expressed not by any overt emotional display but by such symbols as clothes. The expressions of grief did not vary according to personal feelings in the matter. Emotional outlets were provided in various forms of art (painting, calligraphy, drama, music and dance) and amusement (sex, gambling, drinking) which were more or less institutionalized. But these outlets were not allowed free reign, so that the higly formalized social relations were not disturbed. With respect to drinking, a perceptive observer of the Korean remarked:

> Even in extreme drinking, the Korean staggers to his bed rather than reaches to extreme culmination of alcoholic excess by collapsing unconscious on the social scene.[6]

In general, the cultural values reinforced and implemented the other values and held them together in the whole value system. They provided for the accepted display of attitudes and emotions in the routine as well as in crisis situations. Expression which provides emotional release and relaxation can quite easily lead to the subversion of the social structure, since such behavior is ego-oriented rather than collectivity-oriented. But in Yi Korea the subsumption of cultural values under the integrative values served to prevent such a subversion from occurring.

Notes

1. They are: the economic value, political value, cultural value, and integrative value. See T. Parsons and N. Smelser, *Economy and Society* (Glencoe, Ill.: The Free Press, 1956), chap. 2.

2. Robert N. Bellah, *Tokugawa Religion* (Glencoe, Ill.: Free Press, 1957).

3. Arthur J. Brown, *The Mastery of the Far East* (New York: Charles Scribner Sons, 1919).

4. As a contrast, the military in Tokugawa Japan had higher status than the civil officials. See Robert Bellah, *op. cit.*

5. Robert Bellah, *op. cit.,* p. 14.

6. Cornelius Osgood, *The Koreans and Their Culture* (New York: Ronald Press, 1951).

3 / The Chongyok or Book of Correct Change: Its Background and Formation

Perhaps, one of the important intellectual products of Korea was the appearance of the *Chongyok*[a] or the *Book of Correct Change* in the nineteenth century. This book should not be understood as a commentary to the *I Ching*[b] or the *Book of Change*. It is a new book and can be best understood as the counterpart of the *I Ching*. If we call the *I Ching* the *Chou I*[c] or the Chou *Book of Change*, we can call the *Chongyok* the Korean *Book of Change*. The *Book of Correct Change* is very difficult to understand for those who do not have some basic knowledge of the *I Ching*. Moreover, it is filled with complex numerology and *yin-yang* symbols, along with some esoteric mantras.[1] Therefore, it is studied by a few dedicated scholars who mostly belong to the older generation. As an introduction an attempt will be made to provide some background for the origin and significance of this book.

To understand the origin of the *Book of Correct Change* one must realize the background of its author and the predicaments of the Korean people in the nineteenth century. The author of this book was Kim Il-bu,[d] whose given name was Kim Hang.[e] He was born in 1826 in a small village, Dang'gol,[f] which is now known as Namsan-ri[g] in Ronsan[h], and died in 1888. Being a descendant of the thirty-seventh King of Silla dynasty and a son of Kim Lin-ho,[i] he inherited the rich background of Neo-Confucian scholarship. When he was a boy he was greatly interested in the fundamental doctrine of Neo-Confucianism, the study of *Songri*[j] or the Human Nature and Principles, along with the study of Confucian book of Propriety or *Li Chi.*[k] As he grew up he became more interested in the study of the Book of Poetry or *Hsi Ching.*[l] His interest in these books seemed altered suddenly when his teacher, Yi Yon-dam,[m] who was also known as Yi Yun-kyu,[n] asked him to concentrate on the study of the *I Ching* or the *Book of Change*. Kim Il-bu was thirty-five years old when his teacher assigned him to search for the movement of the moon's shadow in the central heaven in the *Book of Change*.[2] After nineteen years of concentrated study he was able to find the movement of the moon's shadow in the central heaven. This finding was described in the *Book of Correct Change*.

The importance of Kim Il-bu's teacher, Yi Yon-dam, should not be under-estimated in the study of *Chongyok*. It must be remembered that Yi Yon-dam was also the teacher of Chae Che-u[o] or Chae Su-un[p], who led the movement of *Donghak*[q] or the Eastern Learning which aroused the conscience of the Korean people at that time. According to Yi Chong-ho, Chae Che-u and Kim Il-bu were called together by their teacher, Yi Yon-dam, to discuss the destiny of Korea and their responsibility to rescue the tradition of the past from spiritual decadence.[3] Since Kim Il-bu was deeply influenced by his teacher, it is certainly probable that Kim Il-bu shared similar ideas to Chae Che-u. It can be seen clearly that the *Book of Correct Change* expresses similar ideas to the Eastern Learning in different perspectives. Moreover, the year when Kim Il-bu was assigned to search for the movement of the moon's shadow in the central heaven was the same year that Chae Che-u was imprisoned and finally executed in Taegu in 1864. It seems to be more than a coincidence that Kim Il-bu's ideas were similar to those of Chae Che-u. Therefore, it is important to understand what Chae Che-u taught if one is going to understand Kim Il-bu's mind in his study of the Book of Change and his writing of the *Book of Correct Change*.

As background, some of the basic doctrines of Chae Che-u, the founder of the Eastern Learning, should be understood. Chae Che-u's doctrines were recorded in his four papers and eight verses based on his own experience of enlightenment or the Great Awakening on the morning of April 5, 1860 when he was thirty years old.[4] These four papers are *Podokmun*[r] or the Spreading the Great Virtues, *Ronhakmun*[s] or Expounding the Great Virtues, *Sudokmun*[t] or the Ways and Means to save people and fulfill the Great Virtues, and *Pulyon'giyun-jang*[u] or Expounding the Mystery of Self-realization Processes. These four papers along with eight verses are found in the Scriptures of the Eastern Learning or *Dong-gyong Daejon*.[v] The motivating force behind the declaration of these doctrines was the self-reliance of the Korean people and the rejection of foreign interference. The Eastern Learning was intentionally coined to assert the national consciousness of the Korean people against Western intrusion through Catholic Christianity. In *Podokmun* Chae Che-u said, "From what I hear from the Western men, they are saying that they will take the wealth and honor for the will of the Heavenly Father. Nevertheless, I have to question their motives, for they set up the churches to conquer the world."[5] It will be noticed later that Kim Il-bu also asserts the self-reliance of the Korean people through the *Book of Correct Change*. Both Chae Che-u and Kim Il-bu agree that the unique symbol of Eastern wisdom is expressed in the Great Ultimate as symbolized in the Korean flag.[6]

However, the central doctrine of the Eastern Learning is the idea of *Innaech'on*[W] or "Man is Heaven or the divine," which has been the corner stone of everything that Chae Che-u preached. This principle is contained in all the major Asian religions[7] and is also expressed in the *Book of Correct Change*. Its purpose was to renew men and reform an ill society—the decadence and corruption of human morality and the economic and political illness of that time were obviously in the mind of Chae Che-u.

Donghak also advocated the idea of *Pogukanmin*[X] or protecting the nation and securing peace for all people. It was interested in the restoration of genuine humanity, peace, harmony and the equality of all men. Moreover, its ultimate goal was to establish heaven on earth or *Ch'isang Ch'on'guk*[Y]. Similar ideas were expressed in Kim Il-bu's *Book of Correct Change*.[8]

One should not overlook the social and political predicaments of the Korean people in the middle nineteenth century when the *Book of Correct Change* was introduced. Korea was almost on the verge of destruction due to both domestic and foreign troubles. In the east, Japan grew in power through *Meiji*[Z] Reform and had already encroached on Korea. In the west, China had dominated Korea for a long time and was still unwilling to release its power. In the north, Russians were expanding their power. Moreover, British battleships had already appeared at Kuge island to exercise colonial interest. Korea became the prey of many powerful nations. In this dangerous moment, domestic illness was beyond description. The officials were corrupt and powerless. The common people were oppressed and exploited by the ruling class. Countless reformers were persecuted and died without achieving anything. Peasant revolts and ideological confusions marked the period when reform and renewal movements such as *Donghak* and *Chongyok* were born.

What is then the *Book of Correct Change?* Why is this book so significant? As has been indicated, the *Book of Correct Change* is not simply another commentary on the *Book of Change.* The *Book of Correct Change* can be considered the final stage of Change, which had been suggested and implicit in the *Book of Change* or the Chou *Book of Change.* Also, the Chou *Book of Change* was suggested in Fu Hsi's *Book of Change,* which proposes Change in the mystical beginning of Chinese history.[9] In other words, Fu Hsi (or Bok-hui[aa] in Korean) first discovered the *I* (or *Yok*[ab] in Korean); King Wen (or Mun-hwang[ac] in Korean), the founder of the Chou dynasty, discovered the *I* on the basis of Fu Hsi and called it the *Book of Change;* and Kim Il-bu discovered the *I* on the bases of Fu Hsi and King Wen and called it the *Book of Correct Change.*

Why is the *Book of Change* considered completed by Kim Il-bu's *Book of Correct Change?* In order to answer this question one must take time to examine both Fu Hsi's arrangement of Change and King Wen's arrangement of Change. The *Book of Change* is usually considered to consist of the 64 hexagrams, judgments and appendixes or Ten Wings.[10] However, the essence of this book is none other than eight trigrams, or *Palkwa*[ad], which are doubled to make the 64 hexagrams.[11] Fu Hsi's *I* or Change is considered to be his arrangement of eight trigrams. King Wen rearranged them to compile the book which is known as the *Book of Change.* Therefore, it is essential to take up the essential constituents of Change or the eight trigrams and examine their arrangements as critically as possible.

According to the *Ta Chuan*[ae] or the Great Treatise, King Wen rearranged eight trigrams on the basis of Fu Hsi's arrangement. As it said,

> When in early antiquity Pao Hsi [Fu Hsi] ruled the world, he looked upward and contemplated the images in the heaven; he looked downward and contemplated the patterns on earth. He contemplated the makings of birds and beasts and the adaptations to the regions. He proceeded directly from himself and indirectly from objects. Thus he invented the eight trigrams in order to enter into connection with the virtues of the light of the gods and to regulate the conditions of all beings.[12]

Fu Hsi arranged the eight trigrams according to natural order. Therefore, his arrangement is often called the natural arrangement of eight trigrams. The second chapter of the *Shuo Kua*[af] or Discussion of the Trigrams seems to explain the Fu Hsi's arrangement: "Heaven and earth determine the direction. The forces of mountain and lake are united. Thunder and wind arouse each other. Water and fire do not combat each other. Thus are the eight trigrams intermingled."[13] Here, heaven and earth are represented by *Ch'ien*[ag] (☰) and *K'un*[ah] (☷); the forces of mountain and lake by *Ken*[ai] (☶) and *Tui*[aj] (☱); thunder and wind by *Chen*[ak] (☳) and *Sun*[al] (☴), and water and fire by *K'an*[am] (☵) and *Li*[an] (☲). The order of these trigrams according to Fu Hsi's arrangement is believed to be as follows:

Diagram 1

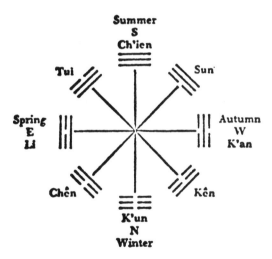

The above diagram of the Fu Hsi arrangement of eight trigrams is also commonly known as the Sequence of Earlier Heaven or Former Heaven. Heaven and earth occupy the central positions of the entire trigrams. The central positions or *Ch'ie*[ao] determine the directions of south and north. The forces of water and fire occupy the West-East axis and carry out the primary function of the trigrams. Thus this axis is known as *Yong*[ap] or function. Here, the

East-West axis is relative to the North-South axis, since the *Yong* deals with the functional aspect of the trigrams governed by the *Ch'ie* or the central position of heaven and earth.[14] To say it in another way, the heaven (*Ch'ien*) and earth (*K'un*) or father and mother, set the order of all things; water and fire (or the middle son and middle daughter) act as the arms of the body to take charge of all affairs of the world. The *Tui* (or lake) and *Ken* (or mountain) also represent the youngest daughter and youngest son. They are united because they are mutually attractive and blend in each other.[15] The *Chen* and *Sun* (thunder and wind) occupy the northeast and southwest axis and mutually stimulate their activities. Therefore, the eight trigrams are well ordered and integrated into a whole cosmic order. This arrangement, or the arrangement of Earlier or Former Heaven, is based on natural order, the order of evolution, which can be illustrated in the following diagram:

Diagram 2

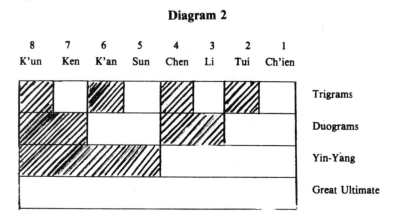

The above diagram shows that the change from the first trigram, *Ch'ien,* to the eighth or the last trigram, *K'un,* is in a systematic fashion based on the binary system. The entire process begins with the Great Ultimate or the Change itself to *yin* and *yang* in duograms, and then to four images which are divided again according to *yin* and *yang,* and finally to the eight trigrams which are further subdivided according to *yin* and *yang.* The process of this natural change can be illustrated in the following diagram which will help explain why Fu Hsi discovered the arrangement of Earlier or Former Heaven sequence:

Diagram 3

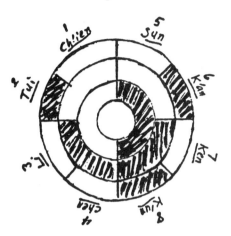

From the above diagram it should be observed that the evolvement of the trigrams begins with one (*Ch'ien*) and moves to four (*Chen*) in a counter clockwise direction, and then from five (*Sun*) to eight (*K'un*) in a clockwise direction. Going backward presupposes going forward. As the *Shuo Kua* or Discussion of the Trigrams says, "Counting that which is going into the past depends on the forward movement. Knowing that which is to come depends on the backward movement. This is why the Book of Change has backward moving numbers."[16] This idea that one presupposes its counter-part is the fundamental principle of change. If one moves forward, it also presupposes its backward movement. If one is to exist, it also requires non-existence.[17] Likewise, the existence of the Earlier Heaven presupposes the presence of the Later Heaven. Since the arrangement of Fu Hsi is the Earlier Heaven arrangement, it also presupposes the Later Heaven arrangement, which is known as King Wen's arrangement of eight trigrams. The appearance of King Wen's arrangement or the Later Heaven arrangement is certainly implicit in the Earlier Heaven arrangement of Fu Hsi.

Before disscussing King Wen's arrangement of eight trigrams, the pattern of change expressed in the natural sequence of Fu Hsi's arrangement can be simply summarized by stating that one is part of the other. Here, one is not absolute but relative to the other, the counterpart of the one. To say it in another way, one is also two, since one is part of the other. Just as one direction presupposes the counter direction, so one is inclusive of the other, the counterpart. Since one includes the other, one is in fact two. Also, two is one since two is none other than one that has the other. In this way the pattern of change can be summarized as one is two and two is also one.[18] This pattern is the basis of understanding the Earlier Heaven or *Sunch'un*[aq] arrangement which includes the Later Heaven or *Huch'iun*[ar] arrangement by King Wen.

The *Book of Change* is based on King Wen's arrangement of trigrams which is quite different from Fu Hsi's arrangement. Diagram 4 is known as King Wen's arrangement,[19] in which *Li* (fire) and *K'an* (water) occupy the central axis, the axis that determines the direction of the entire trigrams. This axis is the *Ch'ien* or the central position of the entire structure. On the other hand *Chen* (thunder) and *Tui* (lake) occupy the axis of East and West, which is usually known as the *Yong* or the primary function of the entire structure. The other four trigrams are placed in four corners, which are regarded as insignificant positions. *Sun* (wind) faces *Ch'ien* (heaven) and *Ken* (mountain) faces *K'un* (earth). There does not seem to be any satisfactory explanation for the Later Heaven ar-

Diagram 4

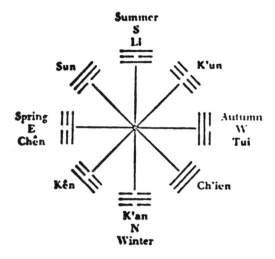

rangement, which has been supposed to be derived from the Earlier Heaven arrangement.[20] One thing that must be remembered in the Later Heaven arrangement is that the East-West axis does not act as the *Yong* or the primary function of *Ch'ie* or the central position of the structure. Rather, *Chen* and *Sun* or East and Southeast take up the activities of *Yong*.[21] In other words, *Chen,* the first son, and *Sun,* the first daughter, take the lead in accomplishing all things in the changing process. Moreover, all the trigrams, except *Li* and *K'an,* are not correlated in terms of *yin* and *yang*. *Chen,* the first son, is related to *Tui,* the last daughter; *Sun,* the first daughter, is related to *Ch'ien* the father; and *K'un,* the mother is correlated to *Ken,* the last son. There is disharmony and disorder of arrangement in the Later Heaven sequence. Nevertheless, it must be the counterpart of the Earlier Heaven arrangement. Both the Later Heaven arrangement and the Earlier Heaven arrangement are inclusive and one in two separate manifestations. Just as one is two and two is one, so the Later Heaven and Earlier Heaven are one but also two. It can be said that the Earlier Heaven means the past and the Later Heaven means the present. However, the past contains the present and present is part of the past. They are one in two different manifestations of time.

Until Kim Il-bu, the Later Heaven arrangement was accepted as the complete and correct arrangement to complement the Earlier Heaven arrangement. Countless commentators in the past had attempted to justify King Wen's arrangement as the perfect counterpart of Fu Hsi and used all possible human imaginations to explain it. Even the *Shuo Kua,* which is traditionally attributed to the writing of Confucius, attempts to justify it.

> God comes forth in the sign of the Arousing; he brings all things to completion in the sign of the Gentle; he causes creatures to perceive one another in the sign of the Clinging (light); he causes them to serve one another in the sign of the Receptive. He gives them joy in the sign of Joyous; he battles in the sign of the Creative; he toils in the sign of the Abysmal; he brings them to perfection in the sign of Keeping Still.[22]

Here an attempt is made to explain the Later Heaven arrangement from the phenomenal manifestation of all things in the universe. The activity begins from the East or Spring, then to the Summer or South, to the West or Autumn and then to the North or Winter. Even though the countless scholars of the *I Ching* has attempted to justify the arrangement from this passage, none of them seemed to succeed in doing so, because they accepted it as complete and gave no thought to the possibility of its incompleteness. It was Kim Il-bu who first came to notice that King Wen's arrangement was incomplete and must be understood only in relation to the complete arrangement. This was perhaps one of the reasons why Kim Il-bu started to search for a complete arrangement following the instruction of his teacher, Yi Yun-dam.

The Later Heaven arrangement is incomplete in relation to its counterpart, the Earlier Heaven arrangement. According to tradition, the Earlier Heaven arrangement was made on the basis of the River Map or *Ho T'u*as (*Hado* in Korean), which was believed to be discovered or revealed on the back of a dragon-horse coming out of the Yellow River. On the other hand, the Later Heaven arrangement was made on the basis of the River Writing or *Lo Shu*at (*Raksu* in Korean), which was believed to be revealed on the back of a turtle. Both are based on myths, though some scholars have attempted to show that they were reconstructed during the period of Yin-Yang and the Five Elements Schools in the later Han dynasty.[23] Whatever their origins, they became important to understand both the Earlier Heaven and Later Heaven arrangements. The River Map is often called the symbol of ten numbers or

Diagram 5

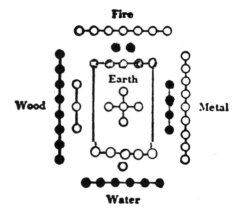

Sipsusang, [au] because its basic numbers are ten. As can be seen, the center consists of five heavenly numbers and ten earthly numbers. The light dots represent *yang* or heavenly character and the dark dots represent *yin* or earthly character. Water in the north is the one of heaven complemented by the six of earth. Fire in the south is the two of earth complemented by the six of heaven. Wood in the east is the three of *yang,* or heaven, complemented by the eight of earth or *yin.* Metal in the west is the four of earth complemented by the nine of heaven. And earth or soil in the center is the five of heaven complemented by the ten of earth or *yin.* There is harmony of *yin* and *yang* or dark and light dots. *Yin* is represented by the dark and even numbers, and *yang* by the light or odd numbers. *Ta Chuan* or the Great Treatise describes the numeral system of this Map as follows: "Heaven is one, earth is two; heaven is three, earth four; heaven is five, earth six; heaven is seven, earth eight; heaven is nine and earth ten."[24] This Map can be understood as the blueprint of a complete world and the potentiality of all possible becomings. This is a perfect paradigm of the changing process in the Earlier Heaven.

The River Writing became the basis for King Wen to construct the Later Heaven arrangement. The River Writing is also known as the symbol of nine numbers or *Gugungsu,* [av] because it consists of nine numbers all together. Diagram 6 is believed to be the reconstruction of the original River Writing. As can be seen in the diagram, water in the north is the one of heaven and complemented by fire in the south which is the nine of heaven. Wood in the east is the three of heaven and complemented by metal in the west which is represented by the seven of heaven. Earth in the southwest is represented by the two of earth and complemented by earth in the northeast, represented by the eight of earth. Likewise, wood in the southeast consists of the four of earth and complemented by metal in the northwest, represented by the six of earth. To summarize, one is complemented by nine, two by eight, three by seven, four by six and five exists by itself. Since odd numbers represent *yang* and even numbers *yin,* the *yin-yang* harmony is not attained in the River Writing at all. *Yin* numbers are correlated with *yin,* and *yang* numbers with *yang.* Therefore, the Writing indicates disharmony. On the other hand, there is an order and harmony in the River Map, where one is correlated with eight, two by seven, three by six

Diagram 6

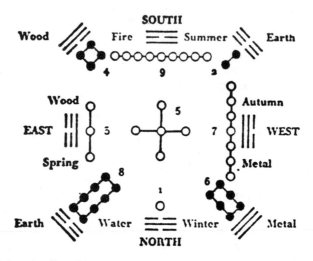

and four by five. Here, *yin* numbers (even) are correlated with *yang* numbers (odd). Again, Kim Il-bu noticed that the Later Heaven arrangement based on the River Writing is disordered. However, one of the most significant observations that he seemingly made was the alteration of the positions of fire and metal in the River Writing. In the River Map, two (*yin*) and seven (*yang*) occupy the south and represent fire, and four (*yin*) and nine (*yang*) occupy the west, representing metal. However, in the River Writing two and seven occupy the west rather than the south, and represent metal rather than fire. Also, four and nine occupy the south, rather than the west, and represent fire rather than metal. In other words, "two-seven" in the River Map is fire in the south, while it becomes metal in the west in the River Writing. Also "four-nine" in the River Map is metal in the west, while it becomes fire in the south in the River Writing. Their positions shifted. Since the River Map is the perfect paradigm of the changing process, the change of their positions in the River Writing is due to the distortion or disharmony of *yin-yang* balance. Kim Il-bu concluded that the basic disharmony and incompleteness of the Later Heaven arrangement, based on the River Writing, was fundamentally due to the displacement of fire and metal in the River Writing. This change of positions was a key to the *Book of Correct Change.*

However, it is important to know that Kim Il-bu did not dismiss King Wen's Later Heaven arrangement, which became the basis for the *Book of Change*. Rather he accepted it as an inevitable aspect of the changing process. He never had any intention of replacing King Wen's arrangement but accepted and completed it. This correction of Change is also a part of the same process which includes both the Earlier Heaven arrangement and the Later Heaven arrangement. That is why Kim Il-bu's *Book of Correct Change* is not the replacement of the two earlier arrangements but rather their completion.

The complete pattern of change then comes from the nature of the changing process. The very process of change itself deals with the former and the latter, or *yin* and *yang*. In other words, one presupposes the other. This is the basic formula of "one in two" and "two in one" relationship. If there is the Earlier Heaven arrangement, there must be the Later Heaven arrangement also. If there is *yin,* there must be *yang*. However, there is also another relationship which is inherent in the idea of "two in one" and "one in two." This requires the third dimension, which completes the unit of change. This third dimension of relationship is important in understanding the formation of the *Book of Correct Change*.

The idea of "two" or *yin* and *yang* is an essential relation of the changing process, but the concept of "three" or trinity is the essential unit of complete change. This distinction must be made, even though they are inseparable in reality. The relationship between two and three is similar to the relationship between one and two. Just as one is in two and two in one, two is in three and three in two. If two (or *yin* and *yang* relationship) is described as the foundation of the changing process, the relation of three is then the completion of that process, because two is complete in three and three is the fulfillment of two.

Why is two completed in three? Change is an act of creativity, which also presupposes the act of destruction as well. The act of creativity is possible because of *yin* and *yang* which are the agents of change. Here, the act of creativity itself is to be understood in terms of three rather than two. The idea of creativity includes what is created, the completion of creativity, or the complete unit of change. To say this in other way, the completion of change as an act of creativity implies the trinity of relationship which includes what is created and what creates through *yin* and *yang*. Two, or *yin* and *yang,* are fundamental agents of change but they are not change if nothing is changed. Therefore, the complete unit of change includes both that which changes and that which is changed or changing. Thus, two is also three because they are inseparable. Just as one is two, two is also three in the process of change.

Since two is completed in three, it can be seen that the third book of change or the *Book of Correct Change* seems to be necessary for the completion of the book of change. The first *Book of Change* was Fu Hsi's, the second was King Wen's, and the third was Kim Il-bu's. The first and second books are completed in the third.

Because three is the complete symbol of two in the process of change and transformation, the *Book of Change* defines "three" as the complete unit of change. This threeness is often known as the three powers or *Samjae,*[aw] which is completed in the eight trigrams. These three powers are often known as the power of heaven, earth and man.[25] Here, heaven and earth are the primordial agents of change, and man is of that change. In other words, man is the child of heaven and earth. Since what is changed (the child) shares two (or *yin* and *yang,* represented by the father and mother), the child (or the three) is of the father and mother, or two; and the father and mother, or two, are included in the third. Here again, two is also three since it is inclusive in the process of change.

Since three is the complete unit of the changing process, everything in the world completes in three. Things begin with birth, expand and then contract. These three stages are known as *Saeng,*[ax] *Chang,*[ay] and *Song*[az] or birth, growth and completion. Kim Il-bu noticed that these three stages were also known in the idea of change. He called Fu Hsi's change or arrangement the first stage, or the stage of *Saeng;* King Wen's arrangement became the second stage, or the stage of *Chang,* and his own arrangement of change became *Song* or the stage of completion. In other words, the *Book of Correct Change* is the third stage, signifying the complete unit of the changing process.

The idea of a third arrangement of trigrams was implicit in the first arrangement by Fu Hsi, as can be seen in Diagram 1. In that diagram the first lines (always count from below) of trigrams are consistent. In other words, from the first to fourth trigrams, or from *Ch'ien* to *Chen,* the first lines are undivided while from the fifth to the eigth, or from *Sun* to *K'un,* the first lines are divided. The consistency of the first lines can be seen more clearly in Diagrams, 2 and 3. Kim Il-bu seemed to notice that the first lines were consistent in Fu Hsi's arrangement, for this arrangement was the first one. According to this kind of reasoning the second arrangement of trigrams by King Wen should have consistency of the second lines. However, the second lines are inconsistent. Kim seemingly understood that the inconsistency in the second arrangement was due to the period of growth. The third arrangement by Kim Il-bu should be then represented by the consistency of the third lines of trigrams. As can be seen, the third lines are consistent in the arrangement of trigrams by Kim Il-bu.

The diagram that follows indicates that the third lines of trigrams from *K'un* to *K'an* are divided, and those from *Li* to *Ch'ien* are undivided. Just as in the first arrangement where the first lines of trigrams are consistent, so the third lines of trigrams in the third arrangement are consistent. Kim Il-bu's arrangement confirms the first arrangement made by Fu Hsi. When the disorder is due to the expansion and growth taking place in King Wen's second arrangement, it is natural to return to the order and harmony of the original, thus completing it. The differences between these two arrangements are certainly obvious. The primary positions of *Ch'ien* and *K'un* have altered by 180 degrees, and *Ken* and *Tui* (the youngest son and the youngest daughter) are placed in the East and

Diagram 7

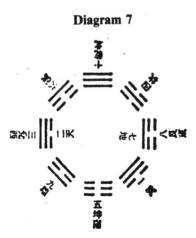

West to take charge of their filial duties as the positions of *Yong.*
Moreover, heaven and earth are added within the arrangement of
eight trigrams. Heaven faces to the west having number two, and
earth faces to the east having number seven. Combining both of
them with the eight trigrams, the third arrangement by Kim Il-bu
has ten symbolic numbers, which are identical with the symbolic
numbers of the River Map, the source of the first arrangement of
trigrams by Fu Hsi.

   As already indicated, the positions of fire and metal in the
River Writing, which becomes the basis for the second arrangement
by King Wen, have shifted from their original positions in the River
Map. The shift, according to Kim Il-bu, has created an enormous
disorder as well as a serious danger of cosmic process. In the second
arrangement of trigrams by King Wen in Diagram 4, the weight of
the arrangement is heavily leaning toward the west. The position of
Ch'ien or father is in the northwestern corner, and that of *K'un* or
mother is in the southwestern corner. As they occupy the western
corners, the entire system is unevenly shifted toward the west.[26]
This unevenness has created a dangerous period of human and
cosmic process until the correction is made through the correct arrangement of trigrams. Bringing fire and metal into the proper
positions and restoring the original positions of the father and
mother, to be the *Ch'ie,* is the primary contribution of the third arrangement of trigrams. Because the third arrangement has restored
their original positions, it is also called the Correct Change
Diagram of Metal and Fire, or *Kumhwa Chongyok Do.*[ba].

Diagram 8

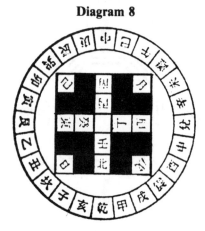

This diagram is the counterpart of the River Map and the River Writing. The twenty-four divisions in the outer circle represent the seasonal changes which are correlated to the inner sequence. The correlation of seasons with the *Book of Correct Change* is due to Kim Il-bu's understanding of Change or *Yok,*[bb] which also means *Yok*[bc] or calendar. According to his Foreword to *Chongyok,* he remarks, "Change is truly change because of calendar."[27] For him change and calendar are identical. It is also said that change is none other than the movement of sun and moon. The relationship between the sun and moon is seen in an analysis of the Chinese character *Yok* or *I,* 易 , which consists of sun, 日 , and moon, 月 , which may possibly come from the old form of 勿 .[28] Restoring the positions of *Ch'ien* and *K'un* or the main axis of cosmos, the correct calendar, that is, the correct movement of sun and moon, is to be attained. In other words, in the *Book of Correct Change* the slanted position of earth is restored to the proper position and the exact seasonal changes are brought into the world. The use of lunar or solar calendars is to be replaced by the *Chongyok* calendar, which does not have any intercalated months or uneven seasons of the year; each month consists of thirty days and a year of 360 days. This astronomical change is one of the new features of Kim Il-bu's prediction.

Kim Il-bu's search for the movement of the moon's shadow in the central heaven was fulfilled in his *Book of Correct Change.* According to Kim Il-bu, the movement of the moon's shadow in the central heaven was concealed in the second arrangement of trigrams and completely revealed in the third arrangement. The cosmic time (or *kalpa*) was believed to be divided into three. The first *kalpa* was the period marked by the first arrangement, which began with Fu Hsi's legendary time and came to an end with the appearance of the second arrangement. The second *kalpa* began with King Wen's second arrangement and ended with the coming of the *Chongyok* period. This marked the third or final *kalpa* and the appearance of the *Book of Correct Change* in 1885. According to Kim Il-bu, *Chongyok* age is the era of the Later Heaven, that will bring ten thousand years of peace and tranquility.[29] The Former or Earlier Heaven era, the era of the *Book of Change,* lasted 2800 years.[30] The Earlier Heaven era was the era of growth and expansion filled with confusion, conflict and disorder. This was the most dangerous era of mankind due to the displacement of fire and metal or the *Ch'ien* and *Kun*. Since the original positions of *Ch'ien* and *K'un* are restored with the coming of the *Chongyok* era, heaven and earth are balanced; peace, equality and harmony of all things are at hand. This is the prophetic vision of Kim Il-bu explicitly indicated in the *Book of Correct Change*.

Notes

1. Mantras in the *Book of Correct Change* deal with the use of fingers to signify the number symbols conveying spiritual meanings. One who knows the mantras is Yi Chong-ho, who taught Korean literature and the *Book of Change* in Gukje College in Seoul and is president of the Chongyok Society in Seoul, Korea.

2. The movement of moon's shadow in the central heaven is a literal translation of *Yongdong Ch'onsimwol* (影動天心月), which seems to mean the movement of sun and moon or the positions of heaven and earth concealed in the *Book of Change*. The significance of this term becomes evident as we see further in the discovery of the new arrangement of trigrams by Kim Il-bu.

3. See his *Chongyok Yong'gu* (Studies in the *Book of Correct Change*), (Seoul: Gukje College, 1976), p. 200.

4. The four papers were written in Chinese and eight verses were written in Korean. The formers were intended for the learned and the latters for the popular group who did not read Chinese characters. However, they are not identical. They complement each other for a proper understanding of the essential teachings of *Donghak*.

5. *Donggyong Daejon* (Seoul: Ulyu Munhwa Sa, 1973), p. 31.

6. See *Ibid*, p. 38.

7. It is often understood that the doctrines of *Donghak* contain the best of these religious teachings. However, *Donghak* should not be regarded as the synthesis of different religions. It has its own unique teachings based on other religions. For the detailed examination of its doctrines, see Paek Se-myong, *Donghak Sasang Kwa Ch'ongdogyo* (Seoul: Tonghaksa, 1956).

8. In the *Book of Correct Change* the idea of the kingdom of God is expressed in a classical term, "the illuminant world" or *Yuri Sege* (琉璃世界).

9. Fu Hsi is believed to be born in 2953 B.C. and died in 2838 B.C.

10. According to tradition King Wen arranged the 64 hexagrams and gave them judgments. His son, the duke of Chou, supplemented judgments to the lines of hexagrams. The ten appendixes or Ten Wings were attributed to Confucius. Scholars question the authenticity of these authors. For a detailed examination on the authorship of the *I Ching,* see author's "Some reflections on the authorship of the *I Ching,*" in *Numen,* Vol. 17, No. 3, Dec. 1970, pp. 200-210.

11. The distinction between trigrams and hexagrams is quantitative. Hexagrams are none other than double trigrams. Thus they are also called *Chungkwa* (重卦). Therefore, eight trigrams are in essence the entirety of the *I Ching*. For more information on the difference between the trigrams and hexagrams, see author's *The Principle of Changes: Understanding the I Ching,* (New Hyde Park, N.Y.: University Books, 1971), Chapter III.

12. *Ta Chuan* II: 2, 1; see *The I Ching or Book of Changes,* the Richard Wilhelm Translation, rendered into English by Cary F. Baynes, Third Edition, (Princeton: Princeton University Press, 1967), pp. 328-9.

13. *Ibid,* p. 265.

14. The distinction between *Ch'ie* and *Yong* must be understood in terms of constitutional and executive divisions. In other words, *Ch'ie* provides the structural foundation of change and *Yong* carries out the constitution or structure of change. Therefore, *Ch'ie* is also known as *Ch'iei* (体位) and *Yong* as *Yong-jong* (用 政).

15. The attraction of the youngest son and the youngest daughter is more emotional since it is closely associated with the passion of sexual vitality. When these two trigrams are united, it becomes the thirty-first hexagram, which is *Hsien* (咸) or Influence. The word means the universal stimulation and is perhaps intended for the sexual union of males and females. It signifies the universal implication of *Hsien* (感), the feeling. In this hexagram, the part of mind (心) is omitted. For the detail account of this hexagram, see The Richard Wilhelm Translation, pp. 122ff. or pp. 540ff.

16. Chapter 2, sec. 3; see *Ibid,* p. 265.

17. The idea of co-existence of being and non-being must be also seen in terms of inverse perspective. It is misleading to conceive that being or *yu* (有) is the other side of *mu* (無). Being is none other than non-being and non-being is none other than being, but they are not identical due to inverse perspective. The technical use of these terms in Taoism and Buddhism has created difficulties in the relationship that we imply in light of the principle of changes. The use of these terms in this particular context is to show the complementary relationship rather than to place a priority of non-being over being. The Taoist or the Neo-Confucian idea of the Ultimateless as non-being is not implied in this context.

18. Again it does not mean that one and two are identical. They are different in manifestation but the same in essence. Just as the one or the great ultimate is none other than two, or *yin* and *yang,* one and two are united without being identical. When we say "one is two," we *intend* to mean the inseparable *unity.*

19. Even though tradition ascribes this arrangement to King Wen, the founder of the Chou dynasty, it is questionable whether he himself carried it out personally. For a detailed discussion, see author's *The Principle of Changes,* Chapter I.

20. Commentators have trouble to explaining the order of this arrangement by King Wen. Even the appendix does not make too much sense, even though it attempts to explain the order in terms of various attributes of trigrams. This will be explained later.

21. This again indicates the disorder. The axis of *Yong* must be the East-West in a proper order. To execute the affairs of eight trigrams in a wrong position creates disharmony and inefficiency of activity.

22. *Shou Kua,* II, 5: See also the Richard Wilhelm Translation, p. 268.

23. See the detail in author's *The Principle of Changes,* Ch. I.

24. Chapter 9; see the Richard Wilhelm Translation, p. 308.

25. The three powers of heaven, earth and man are based on the so-called Chinese trinity. In the trigram the upper line symbolizes heaven, the bottom line earth and the central line man.

26. Yi Chong-ho, *op. cit.,* p. 18.

27. Kim Il-bu, *Daeyoksu* (大易序), which begins with this verse. This Foreword was written in a single sheet in Chinese characters. See also *Ibid*, Appendix, p. 68.

28. See James Legge's translation, *The Yi King* (London: Clarendon Press, 1899), p. 38, note 1: " 易＝日 , the sun, placed over, a form of the old ⺄(＝月), the moon."

29. Kim Il-bu, *Chongyok*, leaf 19.

30. See *Daeyoksu;* Yi Chong-ho, *op. cit.*, Appendix, p. 73.

Appendix

a.	正易	q.	東學	ag.	乾	aw.	三才
b.	易経	r.	布德文	ah.	坤	ax.	生
c.	周易	s.	論學文	ai.	艮	ay.	長
d.	金一夫	t.	修德文	aj.	兌	az.	戌
e.	金恒	u.	不然其然章	ak.	震	ba.	金火正易圖
f.	皆君	v.	東経大全	al.	巽	bb.	易
g.	南山里	w.	人乃天	am.	坎	bc.	曆
h.	論山	x.	保國安民	an.	離		
i.	金麟魯	y.	地上天國	ao.	体		
j.	性理	z.	明珀	ap.	用		
k.	禮記	aa.	伏羲	aq.	先天		
l.	詩経	ab.	易	ar.	后天		
m.	李蓮潭	ac.	文王	as.	河圖		
n.	李雲圭	ad.	八卦	at.	洛書		
o.	崔濟愚	ae.	繫辭傳	au.	十數象		
p.	崔水雲	af.	説卦	av.	九宮數		

4 / East Asian Folk-Religious Explanations of Change: A Sociology of Knowledge Approach

GRIFFIN DIX

Hellmut Wilhelm points out that "the situations depicted in the *Book of Change* are the primary data of life—what happens to everybody everyday, and what is simple and easy to understand"[1] and yet he says the *Book of Change* "poses a problem which we are reluctant to face; we are led into a region in which we do not know the terrain; and which we have forbidden ourselves to enter except possibly in rare moments of imaginative daring." Isn't it odd that what appears so simple—"the primary data of life"—could become such a forbidden region for the modern urban Western-influenced mind? My problem is what kinds of experience could make plausible and even positively compelling the general idea of change that includes specifically the *Book of Change,* the almanac and geomancy, and more generally, the cosmology of traditional Korea. I am taking a Sociology of Knowledge approach to the problem.

A very brief discussion of what "a sociology of knowledge approach" means in this instance may be useful. Let me begin with an analytical distinction between activity and experience. The word "activity" indicates what people do physically. As much as possible an attempt will be made to analyze deculturizing activity. The emphasis is on physical behavior not on what is made of it or even why it is carried out. The utility of this analytical step is certainly to be questioned but in the present case the writer will make the step to emphasize that life in villages involves certain things that are and must be done. They must be done over and over, day in and day out. The necessity of doing these things over and over brings along with it certain experiences.

All experience is constructed using cultural and idiosyncratic interpretive procedures which are constantly being matched up with the pattern of sensory input.[2] Most sensory input is relatively easily matched with its interpretation. The interpretation seems to flow naturally from the external data. But some input is so confusing and so fearful that people seem to create elaborate procedures for interpreting it. They may even rely on experts to tell how to interpret it. For present theoretical purposes, the important point is the assertion that we will make sense out of what the experts say by relating it back to the interpretive frameworks that are used very often. Here is where the distinction between activity and experience becomes useful. The often-repeated daily activities bring to mind the cultural frameworks used in interpreting them; the more frequently will its interpretive framework be called up for use. In other words, common activities are one cause of the frequency of use of an interpretive framework, schemata, frame, etc. If a cosmological or "religious" expert says something, the listener is more likely to make sense out of it by relating it to a commonly used framework. If that is true, then a framework brought to mind very often by a frequent activity is likely to be used more than a framework that is brought to mind only rarely by a very infrequent activity. That this simple-minded little theory or assertion is untested is obvious but will it help explain the common Korean (and by extension perhaps, traditional Chinese) usage of an interpretive framework that is a "region in which we do not know the terrain and which we have forbidden ourselves to enter except possibly in rare moments of imaginative daring"? These very crude analytical concepts are thus related in this way:

The question is what are some of the primary data of life—the things that happen to every rural Korean every day—which do not happen to the urban Western-influenced person? Are not the culturally constructed experiences—these village elaborations on and interpretations of things that are simple and easy to understand—some of the very things that create a positive push toward belief in this "idea of change"?

This paper will first describe what is meant by "the folk idea of change" and point out that it is far from the only folk idea of change in rural Korea. Then it will describe some of the cultural "experiences" of ordinary "activity" in rural Korea which promote belief in this "idea of change."

What is Meant by the "Folk Idea of Change"?

In rural Korea changes in family fortunes are (roughly) attributed to 1) political and kinship ties 2) personal character (cleverness, diligence, laziness, etc.) 3) luck in a general way similar to the Western non-specific attribution and 4) the specific "folk idea of change" which involves many separate belief systems concerning time (for example, the almanac), space (geomancy and the almanac) and social categorization (for example, belief in the magical effect of personal names).

Here are some examples of the "folk idea of change":

1. A poor man says that he is poor because his house is not quite in the right location and direction and he will spend his limited funds to change the house site.
2. A group of men are sitting in a "guest room" (*salang pang*). One remarks that he has not seen many rats around recently. Another says, "Yes, things must be very bad in North Korea now." (Rat [*cha*] is the character for north on the compass.)
3. The village chooses a man to do the village offering to the mountain spirit (*pulak che*) by matching his birth time with the particular year. This randomly chosen man from the Western point of view, takes his responsibility very seriously, carries out all the ablutions and does the ceremony on the exact date and time properly for the village to be prosperous and harmonious in the new year.
4. The village chief tells why a village boy was killed by an automobile on a particular day by looking up his birth date and the day he was killed in a book he has.
5. My family lives with the former village chief whose wife has to carry much water from the well for us. We offer to put in a well but he wants to wait, partly because according to the almanac it is a bad year for putting in a well to the north, the logical place in his courtyard.

6. All the descendants of a man buried over 100 years ago have recently met with some misfortune so the grave site of this man is moved from where he was buried to our village where he once lived.
7. A very pleasant and well liked man dies at age 45 and some attribute his death to his trying to fix the *ondol* heating flues under his floor on the wrong day according to the almanac. One of the village geomancers finds him a grave site that is not very good but miraculously one of the mourners, a kinsman of his, turns out to be a more proficient geomancer and finds a very good site overlooking the village. The good thing about this site is the harmonizing of the grave's direction with the direction of the first and last points where the stream can be seen (*tuksu p'asu*). People say over and over that it proves that a good man will naturally find a good site.
8. Finally, an illustration of the "folk idea of change" may be made from an extended quotation from field notes. In a village nearby was a scholar of high repute in the area. He was a poor farmer only forty-five years old but a descendant of a long line of illustrious scholars. He had excelled in elementary school but because of his poverty had been forced to quit school thereafter. Having turned to traditional scholarship, he had gotten such a reputation that people would come from Seoul and other distant places to study with him. When he could, in the late fall and early spring, he would build himself a hut up in the mountains to avoid his many callers from his own and other villages in order to study. He was most interested in the *Book of Correct Change* (*Chongyok*), a Korean completion of the *Book of Change*, written in 1885 by Kim Il-bu. This rural scholar told the following.

The *Book of Change* is a book to know the future. It knows the future but people only know the present. Only high people in government can see the future and they should all know the *Book of Change*. It is not for us. We must live by our social position (*punsu*). The *Book of Change* is to save people later. The direction and process of the world is bad until the sixth and final change. In each area of the world there are now disasters. We should move to those areas that do not have disasters and avoid them now, before the change. The person who will save us is a sage (*songin* or *taein*). He has to breathe with the Heaven and Earth. If one area goes under water he saves people in that area first. This is the work of the people who study the *Book of Change*. The "later world" will come soon. There will be 360 days just like now there are 360 degrees in the globe. There will be no leap year days. It is all decided beforehand. There are six changes and the next will produce the Heavenly Kingdom (*ch'onguk*). Political leaders, saviors and teachers all have to harmonize their minds (*hapshim hada*).

He looked in the first few pages of the *Book of Change* and read that the sage must unite in himself all the *tok* (virtue) that has been passed down and he said that he will unite in himself all the *tok* that has been passed down from his illustrious ancestors, just as Kim Il-bu, a descendant of a Silla dynasty king, united in himself all the *tok* of his ancestors.

There are four seasons and one must do all the work that has to be done at just the right time. By the *tok* of the spirits (*kuishin*) all the lucky and the unlucky will unite together. If your heart is pure already you live in the Heavenly Kingdom. As the cosmos changes to the sixth stage, people must put on the correct heart. Both of these (individual change and cosmological change) will happen together . . . . In the future there will not be such big changes in the four seasons. The summers will be cooler and the winters will be warmer. The North pole will be warmer and there will not be such differences in each region. The Way (*To*) is *yin* and *yang* and they are right. Just as now, in the future we will not be able to plant any time; there will still be changes. But *yin* and *yang* will almost join. *Yin* and *yang* will mix.

Taking out the River Diagram (*Hado*) and the Water Writing (*Nakso*), diagrams of black and white dots, he explained,

Now all the *yin* (black dots) are in the corners but they will mix with the *yang*. In the world to come the *yin* and *yang* are still connected in rows next to each other but they are mixed. North is winter, south is summer but in the new world things will change positions. For each of the five elements the *yin* and *yang* will join. What is now *yin* will go to *yang* and vice versa. What is heaven will go to where earth is now and they will all join and will breathe together. There will be equality and fineness. One should not try to predict (the work of Heaven) but now we only get 5 or 6 *som* of rice from a *majiki* (200 *p'yong* in this region), and then we will get ten. This is beginning to happen and it was all said 100 years ago by Kim Il-bu in the *Book of Correct Change*.

He went on to show how an alliance ("marriage") between the United States and Korea were predicted and how the power of the United States and the wisdom of Korea would be united to bring harmony to the world. Kim Il-bu reoriented King Wen's alteration of the original Fu Hsi diagram. Among his accomplishments, he placed the originally central axis of Heaven (father) and Earth (mother) back into its central position, almost a necessary reorientation in such a Confucian-influenced society as Korea. He also reoriented King Wen's diagram back toward balance and away from the Westward orientation it had had during the rise and dominance of Western nations. According to my informant, this was a proof and a prediction that now, with the sixth change, a more equitable world order would be established.

What ideas are there in common to all these examples taken from different systems for understanding existence? One might first note that they all include an element of what Carl Jung called synchronicity . . . . "synchronicity takes the coincidence of events in space and time as meaning something more than mere chance, namely, a peculiar inter-dependence of objective events among themselves as well as with the subjective (psychic) states of the observer."[3] If for present purposes one leaves out the psychic state of the observer which was Jung's special interest but which he overemphasized in his discussion of the *I Ching,* one is left with the idea of an interdependence of various elements which make up the reality of any moment. In geomancy there is a continuous interdependence between parent or ancestor and child, in the almanac there is interdependence between time, space, social category and activity, and in the *Book of Change* there is interdependence between all of the events of the moment. But more can be said about the nature of the synchronicity. It is especially involved with a set of discriminations employed to categorize the diversity of time, space and activity. The main idea of synchronicity is that these categories and discriminations are believed to be of the essence of change. They do not merely help label it and understand it, they are it. The attitude underlying these belief systems is a magical one, but it is a magic of proper labeling. Why are these labels not seen as arbitrary and relative, merely more or less accurate depictions of a reality that will always escape the label to some degree?

This magic has much akin to ritual. In ritual an act, if it is done properly, is believed to be efficacious even though there is no visible other person to receive it. In geomancy the almanac and the *Book of Change,* if the proper category is found, and the act that it calls for is carried out, the effect will follow. Geomancy, the almanac and the *Book of Change* are the ritualistic application of a set of categories found in written documents to a reality that is believed to correspond entirely to the proper category, in other words, to *be* the proper category. What accounts for belief in the power of each of these category systems for time, space, and activity? Why should a shared category system, location, and the names for temporal change (a calendar) be believed to have such power of correspondence with a past and future reality that is unseen?

What is the "Push" toward this Type of Belief that comes from Activity and Culturally Constituted Experience in a Village such as This?

Specific Shared Norms

The first activity that deserves emphasis is that of seeing and communicating with the *same people* over and over every day. A result of this activity is that these people come to share a very specific set of norms. One might then expect that each village will be somewhat different and that each region, county, etc., will take on its own social character. This is certainly the folk perception. There are a number of Korean words to describe this phenomenon such as *p'unghyang* or *p'ungt'o*. Although these words have an original meaning of direction of the wind or physical geography of an area, they also take on social meanings. Each region is expected to have its own character and its own customs (*p'ungsok*). In geomancy these are, of course, attributed to the geography itself.

Some widely disseminated principles of Confucianism provide the basic rules by which the shared norms are actualized in interpersonal behavior. Age and generation names are some criteria for the display of respect. Kinship involves some relatively specific obligations, both ritual and economic. There are often disputes over these and the disputes bring the shared rules to mind and clarify them over and over. Under these conditions symbolic action, ritual, can take on a power that it cannot have in more diverse and complex social settings. Since the framework for interpreting symbolic behavior is so shared, a symbolic act can become what we Westerners might, making an erroneous distinction, call a "real" act involving wealth or power. In a Korean village a symbolic, ritual act can have what to us is miraculous, even magical efficacy.

There is a development of a specificity of symbolic meaning which is much more exact and finely tuned than a Westerner is able to understand at first. Since perceptual discriminations are so poorly developed in this area, one does not realize how powerful a ritual act can be. To say something in the proper ritualized manner is to do something very forcefully.

This fine tuning of the meaning of many symbolic actions can be directly applied to the interpretation of cosmic actions that are anomalies such as the above-mentioned early death of a good man. Even without a unitary monotheistic and exclusivist religious prophecy like that of the "world religions,"[4] there is still a problem of the meaning of such an anomaly but it is solved by the ritualistic application of a fine-tuned set of distinctions to the universe. These are expected to have the same force in the universe that careful social distinctions have in social experience.

In peasant societies all over the world there is, in the words of Eric Wolf, a "ceremonial fund" in peasant household economy. Because of the experience of shared precisely discriminating norms that persist in small face-to-face communities, peasants must make meaningful and forceful ritual statements socially. Therefore they expect that ritual statements will also have power when applied to cosmic anomalies.

Discussing Chinese lineage organization, Fredrick Wakeman makes a distinction between "ritual leadership" and other types of leadership and points out that "a clan elder might be a relatively *powerless* creature, chosen for genealogical seniority and approved because he could not use his *powerful* position for selfish ends."[5] But note the anomaly that this powerless creature is in a powerful position. He stands as a symbol for genealogical unity and lineage harmony. His power is used to harmonize and arbitrate the many disputes within his lineage. His personality and force of character may be weak but his ritual power (which is real power) is great because of the shared norms which he symbolizes and manipulates.

Lineage and Family History

Along with the activity of communicating with the same people comes the activity of communicating with them *over long periods of time*. Experience of Korean villages was traditionally, and still is, accurate and finely discriminated in knowledge of family histories, both one's own and those of others. This detailed knowledge sets up the anomalies which are passed over and forgotten as distant history by the modern American and to a lesser extent the urban Korean mind. Not only do most people carry in their heads much knowledge of family fortunes, there are also a few old men in the village who are the recognized historians of the village. Many times when asking detailed historical questions of villagers, vague answers would be given and a referral to talk to one of these men. But these men were noted for their speaking ability and would point out puzzles in family history that other people would ponder and discuss while sitting in someone's guest room on long winter evenings.

When talking with local notables in the region, personal introduction would first be given that included the status, often the character, and the grave site of at least five or six ancestors of the man. This knowledge is socially necessary to place people (something to be discussed in a moment) but it is also known by others who reduce or magnify the members of the present generation by placing them in the context of their ancestors. The present, which the modern and Western mind magnifies, was often traditionally seen as a deviant and sometimes anomalous special case of a much more enduring reality of social position. Where this is the case there is a push toward some kind of explanation for these generational anomalies of change.

Place and Placelessness

Another "activity" to be considered (for those who do stay in villages) is the mere fact of staying in one *place* all of one's life. A third area where rural Korean experience is extremely finely discriminated is that of location. Several anthropologists doing fieldwork in Korea at the same time were all amazed at how finely discriminated is the map of a Korean village. Every small valley has its own proper name. A little bend in a stream forty-five minutes' walk from the village will have a name which is recognized by most village males.

Location and family history are closely connected. When this writer first talked with the village chief, he said that only four lineages in the village did grave-site ancestor worship (above four generations from the living). This seemed to be an important distinction for him and later when it became clear how he looked down on newcomers to the village it was realized how important it was. Only four lineages really belonged because they had the graves of ancestors beyond the "present" four generations here in the village.

A village is a sacred fortress with a sacred boundary and a number of sacred locations near its center. It has a sacred tree on a hill near its center, between the natural hamlets. At the change of years, when a temporal boundary is crossed, the new year is made safe by redefining the village boundary and the sacred mountain spirit shrine. The village offering to the mountain spirit is made by splitting the head of an ox that must be the opposite sex from that of the mountain spirit. The man who is chosen for his propitious birth date makes the offering at the mountain spirit shrines in the dark of night, when he offers the boiled half of the head. Then in the light of morning many village males gather at the boundary of the village, now marked off by sacred rope, twisted in the "wrong" direction and bound with white paper strips. After the offering of the uncooked other half of the ox's head is made, a little food is thrown out beyond the village boundary to appease the dangerous unhappy wandering spirits who are placeless.

The distinction between "placeless" and "placed" is a major social and cosmological distinction. A man must always have a place or a position to be secure and happy. If this is true socially it must also be true cosmologically (the social versus cosmological distinction being one that a Western mind is more likely to apply than was the traditional rural Korean mind). This is in part why the ancestral tablet was traditionally so sacred and important; it was the place for the ancestor to sit while being offered his yearly repast in ancestor worship, a repast which kept the ancestral spirit in its proper place for one year.

The emphasis on being "placed" rather than "placeless" can only be understood by knowing the horrors of being a stranger thrown out of one's natal village; to try and find security in a world where security is almost synonymous with kinship. One of the worst punishments that could traditionally be inflicted on a deviant was expulsion from his village. This would probably bring a life of tenancy or hired labor with people who would be suspicious of one and one's offspring for generations to come.

If discrimination toward geographic and social location was so fine-tuned then it does not seem unreasonable that it could easily be applied toward the location of grave and house sites in geomancy or toward time and direction which were thought of as a single system represented in the almanac. The particular space that a person lived in during and after life could be used to explain anomalous social change because place and placelessness were so important in other social and cosmological realms.

Calendrical Change in the Yearly Cycle

The main economic activity is of course farming. It is a platitude that a peasant who lives by carefully observing seasonal changes and who adjusts his activity so directly with shifts in warmth and light should be vitally concerned with the calendar. But the point deserves some emphasis again in the Korean context. Winters are so cold that essentially all productive activity stops. A man can sleep twelve or fourteen hours a day and spend most of the rest of the day sitting and talking. His body becomes much weaker from inactivity. When spring comes he must suddenly work at extremely physically demanding tasks from dawn until sunset or after sunset. At the first day of spring scholars would write calligraphy that was joyous and optimistic about the growth of *yang* and the many happy events which would soon take place. He would paste the calligraphy on his front gate which would soon be left open as work was begun. He would paste the saying, "Plough the earth and yellow gold comes forth" on the door of his grain storage shed in promise of a good harvest.

Every person's age was directly linked to the calendar in exactly the same way. When the New Year came everyone became one year older and on the first day of spring the scholars would also write "Heaven has added a unit of time and mankind has added a year of age" (*Ch'on chung sewol in chung su*). The linkage between calendrical change and individual change in status, all dependent on Heaven, was pasted on household walls for all to remember. After a man had planted he must very carefully observe the level of water in his paddy. Some farmers had to observe the water level and predict rates of seepage, evaporation and flow, well enough to decide whether another trip to the paddy as much as forty minutes' walk from the village was required on any day. This kind of attention to the detailed changes of nature causes a discriminatory perceptual net which far exceeds anything urban man can easily understand. People in the village would have to predict when the sun would set on any piece of land in any given month and the accuracy of the prediction would be important in calculating the value and types of usage for that land. The shape and configuration of the surrounding mountains could make a crucial difference in the success or failure of a crop on that land. Here again, the day-to-day activities necessitated by village life bring to mind experiences that are a positive push toward the ideas underlying geomancy, the almanac and the *Book of Change*. These activities and experiences are not shared by modern and urban man. It may be objected that Korea and China have had cities for a very long time and many people in them believed in geomancy, the almanac and the *Book of Change*. Rather, activity and experience in pre-industrial cities were very different from that in modern cities, that it was common to return to one's rural place of origin and that the rural basis of much of Chinese and Korean culture were recognized and emphasized.

The Idea of Clear-Cut Hierarchy

The activity of interacting with others is always culturally structured. This activity is not only confined to rural life but is also an urban and modern activity. This writer once talked about the idea of hierarchy with the most scholarly man of a village. This man was not a true scholar in the traditional sense but had studied in a cottage school for over four years and had occasionally studied the classics since then. He was concerned and even upset that the new ideas being held up to villages as "modern" and good were much more egalitarian than the traditional sense of clear-cut hierarchy. He said, "How can you have an orderly society based on an ideal of equality? Equality would mean competition and confusion. Clear-cut hierarchy is orderliness and harmony." Change threatens the clear-cut nature of hierarchy. Where proper behavior was once easily understood and thus easily carried out, change makes for confusion and *shilsu* (serious mistakes in "propriety"). For a powerless peasant change can also bring confusion and disaster in his relations with the outside world. He no longer knows what to avoid and who to choose as patron. Perhaps one goal underlying the folk idea of change is to time change by explaining it as pattern or constant.

The unity of experience that comes with life in a Korean village seeks a unity and clarity of social hierarchy which it does not find. The social hierarchy is constantly changing so the folk idea of change balances off this confusion with a heavier idea that change is within an imperceptible order, a pattern, a constant. The relativizing of change within a broader idea of constancy can make the social order once again turn to *li* (*yeui*), "propriety and ritual," as an image of the essential clear-cut boundaries and distinctions for social behavior. Only if the distinctions are kept clear is social behavior easy.

This essay will close with a quote from one of the classical commentaries on the *Book of Change*. This quote emphasizes the easiness of social behavior within clear distinctions; it emphasizes the idea of *change* paradoxically, as an imperceptible shifting ultimate *order* which determines the success or failure of human events, and it emphasizes that change must be held within the constant orderliness of hierarchy and ritual.

The name *I* (*yok*) has three meanings. These are the easy, the changing, and the constant. Its character is the easy. Its radiance penetrates the four quarters; simply and easily it establishes *distinctions;* through it heaven has its brightness. Sun and moon, stars and regions of the zodiac are distributed and arranged according to it. The soul which permeates it has no gate, the spirit which it shelters has no entrance. Without effort and without taking thought, simple and without error: this is the power. Its power is change. *If heaven and earth did not change,* this power could penetrate nowhere. The reciprocal influences of the five elements would come to a standstill and the alternations of the four seasons would cease. Prince and minister would lose their insignia, and *all distinctions would be shifted;* what should decrease would grow; what should rule would fail. This is change. Its state is constant. That heaven is above and earth below, that the lord faces south and the vassal faces north, that the father is seated and the son bows before him: this is the constant.[6]

Conclusion

The way of thinking that is common to geomancy, the almanac, and the *Book of Change* is foreign to the modern urban

Korean and Western mind because everyday social and physical activity in traditional and rural Korea was and is very different from modern urban Korean or Western social and physical activity. This activity becomes "experience" through mainly culturally constituted frameworks for its interpretation. This paper has discussed five areas of activity—four of which are characteristic of small rural villages but are not as common in modern urban areas: communication with the *same people,* communication with them over *long periods of time,* staying in one *place* most of one's life, and detailed attention to seasonal changes and changes in light and temperature necessary for *farming.* (1) Communication with the same people over and over seems to help cause the experience of very specific shared norms which makes symbolic, ritual activity very powerful because of the shared meanings attached to it. This ritualistic attitude which is socially powerful is aimed at the anomalies and threats of change. (2) Communication with the same people over long periods of time helps to cause the experience of knowledge of changes in family fortunes. These are experienced as anomalies which must be explained. (3) The activity of staying in one place most of one's life helps to cause a very fine-tuned discriminatory net for perceiving location. Not only geographic but also social immobility helps to cause the association of geographic place with social place, for example, of a lineage village in the status hierarchy. In many instances, to move out of that place is to become placeless, without the supports that place entails. Location than becomes important as a source of explanation for anomalies and a way to avoid the threats of placelessness. (4) The activity of farming requires attention and a finely-tuned discriminatory net toward calendrical change and changes in light and heat. The attention to these changes, which are experiences which happen to everybody every day, help to cause the belief that calendrical change has a power of its own which can be used to avoid danger or to enhance the efficacy of activity which is properly timed and placed. These activities and experiences are ordinary everyday occurrences in rural Korea but are not common to modern urban Korean and Western activity and experience. When anomalies in experience are met with, or when an important and dangerous decision or action must be undertaken, an illiterate peasant may turn to an expert to help him. But the basic ideas which the peasant has about these systems for understanding anomalous experience are made plausible by reference to the most frequently employed cultural frameworks for creating "experience" out of common daily activities. By the same token, the ideas underlying geomancy, the almanac and the *Book of Change* are, for the modern urban mind, "a region in which we do not know the terrain" because we have not walked it and in which "we have forbidden ourselves to enter" because we have entered a different experience.

Notes

1. Hellmut Wilhelm, *Eight Lectures on the I Ching* (Princeton: Princeton University Press, 1960), p. 17.

2. Ulric Neisser, *Cognition and Reality: Principles and implications of Cognitive Psychology* (San Francisco: W. H. Freeman and Co., San Francisco, 1976).

3. C. G. Jung, "Forward to the I Ching or Book of Changes" in *Psyche and Symbol: A Selection from the Writings of C. G. Jung,* Violet S. deLaszlo ed. (Doubleday 1973), pp. 228-9.

4. Max Weber, *Economy and Society* (New York: Bedminster Press, 1968).

5. Frederic Wakeman Jr., *Strangers at the Gate* (Berkeley: University of California Press, 1966), p. 15.

6. H. Wilhelm, *op. cit.,* p. 15ff.

5 / Women in a Confucian Society: The Case of Chosun Dynasty Korea (1392-1910)

YUNSHIK CHANG

Fewer societies have had more rigid restrictions on women's social positions and roles than Chosun (Yi) dynasty Korea. For five centuries of imperial reign, Confucian scholars and officials—mostly men—devoted a good deal of time to what one may now call the elite politics of women, aimed at building, according to Confucian teachings, the proper image and rules of conduct for women of noble origin.

In this essay, an attempt will be made to examine the processes of image-building, the ideals derived therefrom, and the actual practices reflecting the image. Information has been derived from a variety of archival and other historical materials, the writings of Confucian scholars, novels, folk songs, and folklore.

As much as possible, original sources were consulted for this work. But this essay is still largely a product of what is commonly known as secondary analysis. Following the appearance of Yi Neunghwa's pioneering work, *Chosun Yosongko* (A Study of Korean Women) in 1936, the succeeding four decades witnessed numerous publications on the same topic. They have not only made the undertaking of this project easier by providing well sorted information but also enhanced the reliability of secondary analysis by presenting a series of common themes which various authors agreed upon as essential to a study of women in pre-modern Confucian ages.[1]

Confucian Ideology and Women

At the very beginning of the Chosun period (1392-1910) those Confucian ideologists who had helped King Taecho, Yi Songkye, to stage a palace coup d'etat sought to establish a new social order according to Confucian ideals. In this context the problem of women's ethics emerged as an urgent political issue. At the root of

the political concerns with the social roles of women was the strong
reaction of Confucian scholars against what they perceived as the
anomic state of the previous dynasty which had been heavily influenced by Buddhism. Seen in Confucian moral perspectives,
Koryo women were far from the ideal; they were almost immoral.
During the period when Buddhism was widely practiced, Koryo
society allowed a degree of freedom within which women could in-
teract with men outside the house in non-family contexts. Women
were permitted to visit Buddhist temples and monks, and to participate in such Buddhist festive activities as *palkwanhoe* or *yon-
deunghoe*. Although one cannot infer from this fact the exact
nature of social freedom women enjoyed before the founding of
the Chosun dynasty, it appears clear from reading Koryo poetry
and 'songs' that women expressed their feelings more freely and
diversely, and were presenting a relatively freer and more flexible
image of themselves than women in the succeeding dynasty. The
Chosun dynasty court directly challenged the legitimacy of
women's social role in extra-family settings instead of merely
criticizing their interaction with men, and thus formulated policies
to separate the social domain of men from that of women. It
stipulated rules of women's conduct, and prescribed male / female
interaction outside the family context.

The Confucian model of woman was derived from the Confucian classics. Various works, which had been read widely by literati
since the introduction of Confucian teaching, before the unifica-
tion of three kingdoms by Silla, became the ideological bases on
which to build a new image of women for the new era.

Such early classics of ceremony and etiquette as *Yeki* (The
Book of Ceremony), *Yohak* (Women's Learning), and *Sohak* (The
Elementary Book of Learning) were printed and distributed widely
by the royal court for the education of *yangban* elite women.
Numerous books written especially for women during the period
from the Han to the Sung Dynasties, including *Yokye Chilpyon*
(Admonitions for Women, Seven Parts), *Yolnyochon* (Biographies
of Faithful Women) *Yohun* (Women's Education), *Yokyoso* (The
Book on Women's Manner and Education), *Sok Yohun* (Further
Women's Education), *Yosaso* (Women's Four Books), *Yokyo-
myongkam* (The Book Women Ought to Read), *Yohyokyong*
(Women's Canon of Filial Piety), and *Yonon'o* (Women's Con-
fucius Analect) were also utilized. As it was state policy to limit

public education to men (exclusively oriented to learning Chinese classics), a great majority of women were illiterate in Chinese scripts. It therefore became necessary to translate those books into Korean and edit them to fit Korean situations.[2]

In 1434, the government ordered the local administrative offices to distribute *Samkang Haengsildo*—a pictorial book designed for teaching three principles of ethics—and to mobilize local literati to teach this book to women in the locality.[3] King Sungchong's (r. 1469-1494) mother herself compiled a book called *Naehun* (Women's Education and Discipline), based on Chinese editions of *Yolyochon, Yokyomyungkam,* and *Sohak,* and published in 1472. In 1481, Sungchong issued a royal decree, ordering that *Samkang Haengsil* and *Yolnyochon* be translated into Korean and distributed widely, so that even common women could learn appropriate women's ways and rectify various undesirable customs. In the 1477 edition of *Kyongkuk Taechon,* the Chosun dynasty legal code, there is a provision that household heads, fathers, and teachers should learn *Samkang Haengsil* in order to be able to teach women and girls about the "women's ways." In 1523, following a royal decree, *Sohak* in Korean translation was printed and distributed by the government.

During the reign of King Incho (r. 1623-1649) *Oryunka* (Songs on Five Ethical Principles) was also translated into Korean and distributed to five provinces. In the year of King Sukchong (r. 1675-1720) *Kyongmin Pyon* (Awakening Folks) and *Kwonmin Ka* (Advising People), written by the Korean scholars, Kim Chongkuk and Chong Chul, were printed by the government and sent out to local towns for daily reading by women. King Chongcho (r. 1776-1800) adopted *Yosaso* (Women's Four Books) compiled by Lady Oh, wife of the well-known scholar Che Jekong, as an official text.

Confucian scholars also complemented the government efforts to educate women by writing, editing and compiling elementary text books on the social role of women. It is worth noting that this issue remained one of the most important subjects of intellectual dialogue among Confucian scholars throughout the Chosun dynasty.

Such active efforts on the part of the government in educating women according to Confucian principles was also well matched by individual families—mostly *yangban* elites—with a rigid family training for girls. Failure to conform was not only construed as a disgrace to a woman's whole family, especially to her parents, but also had legal implications relating to entry into officialdom, and to other members of the family. Accordingly, *yangban* elites paid the utmost attention to the training and education of girls from early childhood. It was a widely spread practice among literati fathers to author a book, usually called '*kyenyoso*' (teaching the daughter), a collection of quotations from Confucian classics relating to the behavior of women.

Segregation of Men and Women

The social hierarchy between men and women in Confucian ethics is primarily based on the idea of *yin* and *yang* as stipulated by the *Book of Change,* and is considered as nature's intractable principle:

> That *yang* is strong and *yin* lenient is the heaven's truth, the principle which is in accordance with the man's way of putting man higher than women.[4]

Thus man is likened to the heaven and woman to the earth; man is the source of cosmos formation, and woman is a submissive element in the whole scheme.

Tongmong Sonsup, the first reader at *sodang,* an elementary school, projects this basic rule into the family system:

> . . . . Indeed, he must be dignified in his condescension and personify the positive heavenly element, while she must be docile in her correctness and thus follow the earthly principle in her obedience. Then the way of the household will be perfect.[5]

The creation of a model woman to conform to this principle, together with the formulation of rules of conduct for women, began by alienating women from men in their social activities. The basic rules on the segregation of men and women may be summarized as follows. From the age of seven a boy should not sit near a girl. When a girl reaches the age of ten she should not roam around outside the house. Should a girl go outside, she should walk on the left side of the road, as a boy walks on the right side. Even among relatives, boys and girls aged above sixteen should not sit close to each other. When a woman gets married, she should avoid showing her face to strangers (men) outside.[6] There are further

details on what a married woman should do. A lady should not
walk around the courtyard during the day, should not go outside of
the middle entrance, and should cover up her face if she goes outside the house.[7]

In short, women should stay inside the house as much as possible. But if they go out, they should not show their faces to men,
thereby avoiding possible contact with them. As early as 1414 an
imperial decree was issued commanding that a noble lady should
wear a lace hat. Covering the face gradually became customary
over the years. Toward the end of the Chosun period even commoners' wives came to wear what is known as *changot,* a long coat.
A woman of pleasure, placed at the bottom of the status scale, also
voluntarily covered her face when she went out. What began as a
status symbol for elite women came to be adopted as a general symbol of the status of women.

Differentiation of the world of men from the world of women
had the direct effect of limiting noble women's activities to family
matters within the house. The principle of man-woman distinction,
in the context of family / house, ultimately resulted in the principle
of husband and wife distinction. *Ye Ki* summarizes the principle:

> . . . . in establishing a home the inside and outside affairs are kept separate.
> The man lives in the outer rooms and does not meddle in the interior; the wife
> lives in the inner apartment and does not interfere in the outside affairs.[8]

In other words, the house / family is related to the outside
world only through the male members of the family, and a female
member can contact the outside world only through a male
member, be it her husband, her brother, or her son. Accordingly, a
woman's power to affect outside events was determined by her
capacity to influence a male member of the family. A wise mother
produced a famous scholar for the outside world, a submissive wife
did her utmost to help her husband pass the civil service examination and become a high-ranking bureaucrat, and so on. The fact
that the women's sphere was limited to the house had significant
implications for their relationships with other members of the family. The principle of male-female segregation, reflected in husband-
wife relationship, became the basis of determining hierarchy within
the family setting.

At the beginning of the Chosun period, it was deemed an

urgent policy issue among Confucian politicians to establish the principle of the distinction between the world of man and the world of woman, and of the superiority of man over woman. The imperial court undertook the task of translating into practice these two basic principles of man-woman relations by regulating such symbolic aspects of husband-wife relations as how and where a husband should welcome his wife after the wedding ceremony.

Prior to the Chosun period, it was customary for a man to move into his wife's house after they were married, and to live with his parents-in-law until their children were born and grew up. The fact that the man moved into the in-law's house was considered a custom symbolizing woman's position as superior. This naturally became a subject of debate upon the founding of the Chosun dynasty, and was severely criticized by Confucianists. Chong Dochon, who masterminded the overthrow of the previous dynasty and was responsible for founding a new monarchy on the basis of Confucian ideologies, had this to say:

> If a man moves into his wife's house after he married her instead of following the rite of *chin yung* - the man receiving his wife at his own house - the wife relies on her parents, and treats her man rather lightly, and becomes arrogant by day, and eventually revolts against him, and degrades the family by reversing the superiority and subordinate order.[9]

It was not, however, easy to change an age-old custom overnight. The royal court imposed this new rule first on the royal families, and expected that others would follow in due course. It appears that reversing the custom regarding which family acts as the receiving party at the wedding and domiciles the couple thereafter took more than three centuries to change. Yu Hyungwon, a well-known Silhak scholar (1622-1673), as late as the seventeenth century, comments on the difficulties in practicing the new custom:

> In these days, the royal families all practice the rite of *chin yung*, but the *yangban* families still tend to follow the old custom of having their married son stay at the in-law's place. Therefore, instead of saying, acquiring a wife, people still say that man enters a wife's house, which clearly defies the principle of man-woman relationship by having the *yang* element following the *yin* element. We should therefore correct the errors by following the proper rites, thereby rectifying the man's way.[10]

This issue continued to be problematic throughout the dynastic period, and efforts were made to regulate those men who returned to the wife's home.

Such formality associated with the wedding ceremony was only a prelude to the more substantive principle regulating the relationship between a man and a woman within the house. Confucius stated the basis of this relationship when he put forward what was later known as the principle of "three followings:"

> The wife as a rule is expected to bend, and is not to have a will to rule or self-govern. There is a principle of three followings. In your own family, you follow your father. When you are married, you follow your husband. When the husband dies, you follow your son. At no time do you act and achieve on your own.[11]

In short, "to follow" was interpreted as the utmost virtue of woman in Confucian ethics. Under the premise that a woman does not act and achieve on her own, she was expected to deny any positive element of her own will.

The principle of "three followings" presents three images of woman corresponding to three stages of the life cycle. Each image is based on "woman's way" as it circumscribed her relationship to the male counterpart she encounters in each stage. We will therefore go through these stages, discussing the respective ideals of women in each.

Filial Daughter

Before marriage, a girl was expected to follow her father, or parents. Following one's parents is more generally known as an act of filial piety. Filial piety, in the words of Yi Neung Hwa, is "considered as the foremost form of human action, and the ultimate source of all virtues."[12] The original meaning of the ideal of filial piety, of course, derives from the teachings of Confucius. According to Confucius, "filial piety is the cause of human virtue. All the teachings originate from this."[13] In answer to his disciple, Sam, Confucius defined filial piety as follows:

> One's body, hair and skin are all received from one's parents. That one should not leave them unclean is the beginning of filial piety, which will be completed by following the Way and gracing one's parents by making one's own name known to the succeeding generations.[14]

One's body, one's very physical existence, was seen as originating from one's parents, and accordingly one did not act on one's own behalf, but on behalf of one's parents.

A filial son found his parents in himself, and himself in his parents, through devoting himself to his parents selflessly. Confucius explained the methods of filial piety to Sam further:

> Parents should be served with the utmost respect. They should be made happy when they are taken care of. When they are sick you should worry. If they die, you should express utmost sorrow. When you observe a memorial service you should do so with utmost solemnity. Only when these five forms of service are complete can you say you have done the filial duty.[15]

The ideal of a filial son is clearly illustrated in some of the widely cited stories, those used by parents to teach the principle of filial piety to their children. In one, a filial son finally moved heaven by his well-known piety and thus was able to catch a trout for his father in a frozen river. In another, a man found a bamboo shoot in the snow as a reward for his devotion to his mother.

During the Choson period, the royal court made it a policy to reward filial acts by a son or daughter by building an arch or raising a flag before his or her house so that others could emulate the acts, thereby enhancing the moral standard. Chosun Dynasty Korea produced many filial daughters as well as many filial sons. Numerous books were compiled detailing such activities, although not all of these records have survived. The *Veritable Records* recorded the names and acts of filial sons and daughters, from which one can clearly see the desired image of a filial daughter emerging.[16] A model daughter would shield her father with her own body to protect him from an attacking thief. Another filial daughter cut her finger for her father's incurable disease.[17] The best example of an ideal filial daughter is depicted in the Story of Simchong, a daughter who sold herself to a fisherman as a sacrifice to the *imtang* river, in return for three hundred sacks of rice to be used as an offering for a Buddhist ceremony to open the eyes of her blind father. Pure, selfless devotion to parents was the theme of this story.

Most of the known stories about filial daughters do not concern girls from rich or noble families. They are about the daughters of rather poor literati or commoners. It was expected that noble parents would have filial daughters, but they were not frequently the subject of stories. In noble families, the sacrifice of a daughter was rarely necessary. Extreme situations, more likely to arise in commoner families than in noble families, perhaps provided more opportunities for the sacrificial behaviour considered exemplary of the ideal filial daughter. It should also be noted that filial piety on the part of a daughter was a spontaneous act of free will to cope with extreme situations. This contrasts with the case of a virtuous woman of fidelity, or a filial daughter-in-law, whose relations with her husband or father-in-law were regulated in part by legal codes. Such codes were more rigidly enforced for noble women than for others. Thus, filial piety was an ideal that a girl in a noble family learned about during her childhood, but its practice was usually reserved until after her marriage when she would be expected to practice it towards her parents-in-law. In fact, *yangban* elites were more concerned with educating their daughters to prepare for whatever they would have to face in their future husband's houses, for how they would behave there would directly reflect upon their parents. The noble family, then, typically produced a good daughter, not necessarily a filial one, to marry a man whom her parents chose for her, and became an ideal woman in the in-law's house. Once a girl married, she was no longer considered a member of the family. An old saying expressed it rather well: "A married daughter is an outsider to her old family."

Adolescence, for a girl of noble origin, was the period of education for married life, while for a girl of humble or common origin it was the period to practice the principle of filial piety.

Obedient Wife: Three Faces

After marriage, a woman followed her husband rather than her father. It has already been mentioned that the principle of husband-wife distinction differentiated the domain of a wife's activities from that of her husband's within the family setting. The expectation that the wife ought to follow her husband was taken to mean that neither husband nor wife should interfere with the other's activities.

In Confucian philosophy, forming a couple is considered the beginning of human ethics. From the *Book of Change* we learn that only after there is husband and wife could there be father and son.

In *Ye Ki,* the husband-wife relationship is considered the basis of all other human relationships: "If there is no distinction between husband and wife, there is no son's respect and service for his father."[18]

As a reflection of the importance of the husband-wife relationship, regulations regarding the conduct of the couple were minutely detailed in writings, and were governed by various legal sanctions in Chosun Korea.

The essence of "the woman's way" was perhaps best expressed by Yi Neunghwa:

> The wife must regard her husband as heavenly; what he does is an heavenly act, and she can only follow him.[19]

The wife was expected to carry out this idea in three ways: 1) by following her husband actively to assist him; 2) by following her husband passively, and not objecting or revolting against him, and 3) by following her husband ultimately, devoting her life to the man she married.

a) Active Following

Since the wife's domain is ideally inside the house, whatever assistance rendered to her husband was considered as inside help. Numerous folktales immortalized those wives who helped their husbands become famous by helping them from inside. There was a wife who helped her husband get through the difficult period of preparing for civil service examinations so that he finally became a top-ranking government official. Then there was a wife who helped her husband repent his wrongdoing and start a new life. An ideal wife found it her duty to encourage her husband to take civil service examinations by reminding him that that was the only way for a man to make himself good.[20] Women who rendered selfless assistance to their husbands for their future were frequently idealized in popular novels during the Chosun period.[21]

Not all wives who helped husbands to make their name in the world always succeeded, however. Whether a wife becomes famous outside the house depended almost entirely upon what her husband did with her help. A letter written by lady Samuidang Kim (1769-?) to her husband, who failed a civil service examination, describes well the difficulties she had to face in supporting her incapable husband:

> Last year I prepared your food by selling my hair. This spring I sold my *binyo* (an ornamental bar for hair) to raise money for your trip. Even if all my possessions may be gone I should not let you be short of travel expenses. Please do not worry about home, and do succeed in writing the examination.[22]

More men failed at the civil service examinations than succeeded. Many men from noble families tried their luck at the examination without success until exhausted. Those literati who gave up hope of making it to the imperial bureaucracy through this channel usually opted for book reading—the only alternative to obtain an administrative job. Idle literati read Confucian classics without paying much attention to family finances, which were usually left to the wife to take care of. A man of noble origin was not supposed to engage in farming. It was his "trade" to read Confucian classics. He was not to touch coins, nor to ask the price of grain.[23] Unless the man inherited substantial land from his father he had to remain poor. Even those with land often lacked knowledge of how to manage it and therefore met disaster. The practical meaning of all this was that the wife had somehow to support her book-reading poet-husband and provide for their children's maintenance and education. A famous *silhak* scholar, Hong Daeyong (1731-1784), criticised the situation with unkind words:

> When one's luck comes to an end, a *yangban* man in extreme poverty sits empty-handed, without ever taking a hoe. If he ever decided to do something substantial and engage himself in dirty work, other *yangban* friends would all laugh at him as if he were a slave. As a result, there are too many idle hands and too few producers.[24]

b) Passive Following.

There is a limit to what an assiduous wife can do for her incapable husband. Given the principle of husband-wife distinction, she can only render passive service to her husband, not interfering with his activities or revolting against him. In serving the husband, the wife was not to object to his behavior, except for that which the world would not approve. Any form of challenge to a husband's authority was not tolerated. There were regulations regarding seven sins which a wife should not commit.[25] If she did, she was liable to be deprived of a wife's status and sent back home. They were: 1) disobedience to her parents-in-law, 2) barrenness, 3) infidelity, 4) jealousy, 5) incurable disease, 6) talkativeness, and 7) stealing.

This idea of seven sins reflects traditional values, and may be considered a mechanism for encouraging and promoting the ideal image of woman in traditional society. But more directly, these ideas reflect the vulnerability of woman vis-a-vis man. Vulnerable as women were, divorce never became an institutionalized act for the nobility.

There was a strong folk ideology emphasizing the value of a couple "growing old together." Furthermore, no divorce law existed. One could only appeal to the king through the royal court for permission to divorce. If the request was judged unjust, the applicant could be subject to court punishment. A woman could also make an appeal to the royal court if she deemed the act unjustified. There also were three rules which stipulated the conditions under which divorce was not granted: 1) if the wife had no one to rely upon once she was divorced; 2) if the wife had spent three years in mourning of her parents-in-law; and 3) if a family that was relatively poor had become prosperous since she married into the house. On the other hand, a peasant couple, if necessary, simply discussed the ill-fated marriage and agreed to end it by jointly signing a document (*sajong paui*), or by cutting off a corner of the collar of the jacket each was wearing as evidence for the agreement to divorce (*hwalkup hyuso*). But divorce was not widely practiced at any status level. As late as 1930, the proportion of the ever-married women in each five-year age group above twenty that was divorced was less than one percent. While a woman was relatively safe from divorce, she was not necessarily free from such forms of desertion as the husband taking a concubine.

Concubinage was a legalized institution. A man was free to find a concubine as long as he could afford to support two families, and the wife more-or-less accepted the fact. One of the most justifiable reasons for a man having another wife (concubine) was barrenness. Childlessness was usually blamed on the wife, regardless of the true reason. Although the law originally intended concubinage only for those men who did not have children the practice became widespread among *yangban* elite men. In many ways, men were not satisfied with wives who approached closely the Confucian ideal. They idealized another type of woman—more open, carefree, less formal, romantic, and more intimate with their

outdoor world. In fact, Chosun dynasty men had two models of
woman which they established by dividing women into two classes:
those who marry, and those who do not. The former fit the model
with which this essay is mainly concerned; the latter met the needs
of men for entertainment which the women confined to the house
could not provide. Since men interacted with their wives at a
distance, and wives were expected to serve their husbands as if they
were guests, avoidance and formality penetrated into what could be
the most intimate of relationships. In many cases, a concubine filled the position of entertainer within the family. In many folktales,
a wife forgave her husband's concubine for her beauty and perhaps
sensuousness, which she admitted not possessing. "Any man will
fall for a woman like that," she reasoned.[26] Jealousy and tension
between two wives was then a built-in element in the family system,
and the wife was expected to overcome her emotion or jealousy
without showing it. Expressing jealousy would have inevitably
resulted in a challenge to the husband's authority, the very principle which formed the backbone of Confucian family ethics.
Women in general overtly accepted the two-wife system.

Numerous poems written by *yangban* women at home describe
their suffering. Folk songs sung by commoners' wives were perhaps
more direct in expressing their hatred toward concubines. They all
hated concubines, but they did not blame their husbands.[27]

c) Ultimate Following.

The ultimate test of woman's following was in the third sense,
devotion to one man. According to Confucius, there could not be
two husbands as there were not two suns in the sky, hence the principle of one husband only. Once a man and a woman establish a
couple's bond a woman could never sever the bond. The principle
of one husband only consisted of two basic rules: a woman was not
to commit adultery, nor to remarry when she became a widow.
When a married woman committed an act of adultery, it was considered the most unforgivable act, and received the least sympathy
from others. A woman's adultery, as mentioned above, was one of
the "seven sins." The act of infidelity not only put her to shame,
but also defamed her entire family. In 1495, a proposal was made
to the government to put to the most extreme punishment those
women who committed adultery, together with their sinful part-
ners.[28]

But the meaning of woman's fidelity was much broader than committing adultery. The infidelity of women, especially among the *yangban* elites, included adultery in a symbolic sense. A widely cited story should illustrate the point. There was a women who, during the war, was escaping from approaching enemy soldiers. She had to board a boat which was already full. Given the difficulty, the boat owner gave her a hand to board. Upon realizing that a strange man's hand touched her body, she took out a knife and cut off the arm which the man touched. Regardless of the authenticity of the story, it was popular and frequently recited as an example of the model woman who knew how to practice the principle.

Chosun Dynasty Korea, as it was represented by learned men, upheld the principle of woman's fidelity even during the situations of national crisis such as the Japanese invasion (1596-1603) and the Chinese invasion (1637-1639) that followed. Any form of foreign invasion usually produces innocent victims. The most notorious one is the case of those women who were captured—and most likely raped—by the invaders. After the war, those women who resisted the offending invaders with death were commended as faithful women *(yolnyo* or *cholbu).* But those who were not prepared to die had to go through additional hardships. The Chinese invaders, especially, made a point of capturing women for whom they would later ask ransom. From the point of view of the Confucian moralist the mere fact that a married woman, especially one of noble family, was captured by an enemy soldier was equivalent to her having lost chastity. Those *yangban* elites who subscribed to this view naturally raised a question of whether they should bring back wives or daughters-in-law lost during the war by paying ransom. This issue became one of the most important subjects of long-lasting debate.

One high-ranking group of government officials argued that since many women lost their chastity by coercion in difficult situations, they should not be considered unfaithful. If requests to divorce women in enemy's custody were granted there would be little incentive to try to bring back their wives. Many women would become grudging ghosts in a strange land. The other group, on the other hand, retaliated by saying that if a new divorce law were to be implemented, there would surely be women with a grudge. They argued that for the government to deny men's requests to remarry because of a lost wife would be against the idea of justice. The imperial court, caught between two polarized views, decided to com-

promise by opting for a third alternative. The law remained un-
changed, and the question of whether to bring back the lost wife or
not was left to individual discretion. One minister, Choe Myungkil,
who advocated a change of law in a more humanistic direction,
rebuffed the compromised solution by pointing out that the compromise itself recognized two different laws for the same issue, and
believed this to be improper. In the end the compromise, then called the multiple solution, prevailed with the approval of the king.
The two ideas on the fidelity issue—the supremacy of fidelity which
needed to be sustained even at the expense of a woman's own life,
and humanism which took into consideration crises over which the
concerned parties did not have much control - survived through the
compromised position. But later historians were not in accord with
the advocates of change. In criticising the argument forwarded by
Choe Myungkil, the *Veritable Records* of the Incho period
(1628-1649) had this to say:

> That the royal subject serves only one king, and the wife does not serve two
> husbands is the basis of the fidelity rule. One could understand the difficulty
> that the captured woman had to go through. But to save life rather than
> fidelity in a moment of crisis is a disgrace to the tradition of the nobility.
> Those women who erred should have severed themselves from the husband's
> families. Choe Myung Kil was clearly wrong in arguing for the multiple solu-
> tions by misjudging the whole issue. His act of destroying the country's
> folkways which existed for two hundred years was owing to his perception of
> this country as uncivilized.[29]

In 1648 it was proposed that sons of captured wives be treated
as sons of remarried women. Although this proposal never
materialized, the Confucian idealists recognized an historical error
in not upholding the fidelity rule, and hoped to rectify it by making
the rule more rigid. It gradually became the ultimate goal of women
to guard fidelity even if it meant the loss of life. The fidelity rule
gradually turned into a religious belief.

The guardianship of chastity is an issue directly related to the
problem of the remarriage of widows. On the basis of the principle
of not serving two husbands, widow remarriage was strictly
restricted. Although the prohibition of widow remarriage was not
legalized, restrictions were imposed on widowed women all the
same. As early as in 1406, a high-ranking official, Ho Ung, of the
Department of Justice, said in his recommendations on new
widow-remarriage regulations:

The husband and wife relationship is the foundation of human ethics. Therefore, there is the principle of three followings, which reasons against widow remarriage. Nowadays, wives of men of nobility tend to marry twice or three times at the request of their parents upon the death of their husbands, and do not even feel ashamed of losing fidelity, thereby degrading folk morality. It is therefore my humble wish and request that those women of noble origin who marry three times should, according to the law of the previous dynasty, be registered in *chanyo-an* (the list of the names of women who lost their fidelity) in order to correct the ways of ladies.[30]

King Taechong (r. 1401-1418) immediately adopted the proposal, and declared that "sons of remarried women shall not become high ranking officials in the administration." Sanctions against remarriage were not directed to the remarried woman directly but rather to her sons, by depriving them of opportunities for upward mobility. Blocking avenues to officaldom for their sons was in fact a more extreme punishment to women in Chosun Dynasty Korea than any sanctions against the mothers themselves. The third principle in the doctrine of three followings was that the mother should follow the son. As discussed above, the son was not only the source of comfort for his mother's old age, but also an expression of herself. The son was the utmost achievement of his mother. That her son's path to the prestigious official position was obstructed almost implied taking away the reason for his mother's existence.

From the early days of the Chosun period, the government made nation-wide efforts to promote the idea of fidelity, and rewarded those women who did not remarry and who overcame various difficulties. In 1477, *Kyungkuk Taechon* stipulated that "sons of remarried women who lost chastity, together with sons of concubines, may not take the civil service examinations for *munkwa, saengwon, chinsakwa.*" This provision completed the legalization of the government order which originated from King Taechong. By thwarting the son's opportunity to enter officialdom, the government in fact closed down permanently the possibility of the entire family's prosperity. It therefore became an iron law that once-married women of nobility remained forever faithful to a dead husband, and never remarried.

The problem of widow remarriage is related to the principle of fidelity but is different, in nature, from the problem of losing chastity in time of crisis. What was at issue here was how to generalize the principle of the fidelity of women. The Confucian scholar's official's logic was that the remarriage of widowed women should also be considered a loss of chastity. The immediate implications of this logical extension was that a woman who lost her husband, say three days after marriage, would be forced to remain unmarried since marriage itself was an act of commitment to a man. In an extreme case, a bride who received a letter of agreement from the bridegroom's family after engagement was also considered as having been committed to the future husband, and was expected to remain unmarried for the rest of her life, should her betrothed die before marriage. The *Veritable Records* also recorded numerous cases of those widows who never remarried. The ideal form of guarding chastity was for the wife to follow the dead husband by ending her life after three years' mourning. *Yolnyochon* abounds with stories of women who met this requirement.

The prohibition of widow remarriage remained a serious social issue throughout the dynasty period until the custom was abolished at the end of the nineteenth century. In 1497, twenty years after the promulgation of *Kyungkuk Taechon,* a local school instructor (Song Hondong) presented a petition to the king, bringing to his attention the "unnecessary hardships imposed upon widows by prohibiting them from remarrying." The petition, which subsequently became a famous historical document, reads:

> Prohibition of the remarriage of widows is intended as a means to enhance morality, and to uphold honour. But food and man-woman relationships are the greatest human desires. Therefore a man wants to have a wife, a woman a husband. There is the principle of three followings, which is a teaching by the book of ceremony. Yet there is a woman who became a widow three days after the wedding, or a woman who became a widow a month after the wedding, and there are women who became widowed at the age of 20 or 30, and they are expected to preserve their chastity, remaining faithful. But when a widow does not have brothers or sons to protect her, she may be raped on the street, or someone may climb over the fence, and she will lose chastity involuntarily. I therefore beg of you to permit women who become widowed before the age of 30 to remarry.[31]

Having recognized the significance of the petition, the King called a meeting of ministers, in spite of the relatively low status of the petitioner. As had been the case with the issue of the captured women, opinions again were divided. There was a group of high-ranking officials in the court who more or less agreed with Song's argument and recommendations. They argued that those young widows who could not possibly live alone, while preserving chastity, should be allowed to remarry, and that offspring of widows

should be permitted to enter officialdom in any rank below that of
chonjik, thereby letting wise and capable men enter the administration. They also argued that even the regulation in the *Taechon*
should have some flexibility in certain situations. But the opinion
of the majority was still that "it is impossible to change the content
of *Taechon* which has been in existence for almost 100 years for the
enhancement of morality and the cultivation of pure customs."[32]
Against the humanitarian view which emphasized the vulnerability
of women, the orthodox idealist was adamant in upholding the
traditional Confucian moral standard. The following citation is
representative of this opinion:

> In our country, it is of prime importance to teach *ye* and uphold *cholui.*
> Widow remarriage is a bad custom left over from the previous dynasty. But
> many *yangban* families let remarriage happen. Therefore, King Sung-chong
> prohibited the recruitment of the offspring of remarried widows to high-
> ranking administrative jobs, in order to establish proper customs. We cannot
> possibly go along with the recommendation that we change this beautiful law
> authored by our king.[33]

The majority went for the continuity of the past, protecting the
sanctity of the law. The changing of old doctrines was usually interpreted as a challenge to tradition, which was taboo among Confucianists. This tendency in general had prevailed among intellectuals
in Chosun Dynasty Korea since the teaching of Chu Hsi, known as
Neo-Confucianism, became the state ideology. Although there
were occasional criticisms levelled against "the most formalistic,
nominal regulations ever," serious challenge never arose until the
time of the enlightenment movement toward the end of the Chosun
period.

The fidelity rule was not as rigidly imposed upon commoner or
lower class women as it was upon women of noble birth. From the
available historical documents, it appears that remarriage was
relatively free among commoners. Nevertheless, even among commoner women the adoption of the fidelity rule as a desirable moral
principle was encouraged, though not enforced. There is evidence
of women of humble origin who distinguished themselves by
following this most difficult regulation.

A *silhak* scholar in the 17th century, Yi Ik, made the following—almost cynical—remarks about the state of the fidelity rule in
Korea:

Our country has one beautiful custom which China does not have. That is, even women of low status judiciously keep chastity by not remarrying. This must be due to the state law prohibiting the offspring of remarried women from entering the officialdom. The virtue of noblemen lies in the Way, while the virtue of men of humble origin lies in modesty. But people only respect the Way, not modesty, and as a result, the country's customs become indiscriminatory, even offspring of humble origin are foolish enough to abide by the fidelity rule, although they could not become government officials in the first place. How far-reaching moral education could be. This is all due to the king's leading.[34]

One of the most famous novels of the Chosun period, the story of *Chunhyang,* idealizes a *kisaeng,* or entertainer, attached to a local country office, who overcame great difficulties in order to serve only one man to whom she had given her word of honor. One historian maintains that after the mid-Chosun period the fidelity rule, together with prohibition of widow remarriage, was a custom taken for granted among women of all classes.[35]

Filial Daughter-in-law.

With an extended family system, a wife in Chosun Korea not only served her husband, but also her parents-in-law if her husband was the first son. Once a woman was married to a man she was no longer a member of her family of origin. She began a new life with new duties and responsibilities in her husband's family. One of the most important new duties was to take care of her parents-in-law.

Naehun says:

The son may really fall for his wife. But if parents are displeased with the daughter-in-law, the son should abandon her. Or son may not like his wife, but if parents are pleased with her, he should be happy with her.[36]

In other words, a son's loyalty to his parents was expected to supercede his loyalty to his wife. A daughter-in-law should therefore serve her parents-in-law as if they were her own parents. Expectations regarding the behaviour of filial sons were applied to daughters-in-law with equal intensity. *Naehun's* stipulations on how daughters-in-law were expected to serve parents-in-law were most detailed:

In serving parents-in-law, you should never disobey. If they ask you to eat food you might find to your dislike, you should still try it willingly. If they give you a cloth which you were not willing to try on, you should nevertheless wear it, and wait on them. If parents ask you to do something other than what you are doing now, you should follow them even if you are not willing to do it. Only when you are through with it, you may resume what you were doing before.[37]

Selfless services to others in the husband's family was what the filial daughter-in-law's life was all about. While the filial piety rule had the element of spontaneity or voluntariness when applied to a woman's own parents, there clearly was an element of coerciveness in the same rule applied to the in-law relationship. Although it was expected that a daughter-in-law would serve her parents-in-law in the way she would serve her own parents, the two relationships were basically different. In particular, the relationship between the daughter-in-law and mother-in-law was a relationship between two women to whom one man's loyalty concurrently was called upon. Two women in the same household inevitably competed for the power to control matters relating to indoor affairs, and the mother-in-law was likely to exercise her authority as the mother of the household head. In this sense tension was a built-in aspect of the extended family system, and no matter how persuasive the rule was with its emphasis on spontaneous and voluntary service to parents-in-law, conflict became an outstanding feature even if, ideally, such tension would not be manifest on the surface.

There is a common expression describing the particular relationship between mother-in-law and daughter-in-law, namely *sijip-sali,* living in the house of in-laws. *Sijipsali* implies difficulty in living in the husband's house, difficulty arising from a subtle woman-to-woman relationship and the hierarchal nature of that relationship. Since men were expected to stay away from indoor affairs in the house, the two women concerned had to resolve whatever conflicts arose from living together in a small space. Given this structural constraint inherent in the household, the doctrine of the filial daughter-in-law inevitably had its limit. Spontaneity from a daughter-in-law in giving service to her parents-in-law was not something one could expect as a matter of course, and there inevitably was a felt need for enhancement of the parents-in-law's authority—especially that of mother-in-law, and for obedience. The seven sins, one of which was disobedience to parents-in-law, should be understood in this context. Numerous examples of filial daughters-in-law were recorded in various places like the *Veritable*

Records, and in individually authored books. The stories are rather similar to those of filial daughters or sons. Since the element of affection is more or less absent in this case, the fact that the dynasty produced so many filial daughters-in-law is eloquent evidence of the way in which parents trained their adolescent daughters according to the book of rites, so that they might properly fulfill this role. There also is a book by an anonymous author on daughters-in-law who failed to become filial. The unfilial daughter-in-law, however, never became a political issue in the way fidelity and widow remarriage did.

While a daughter could be a filial child only so long as she lived with her parents, the duties of a filial daughter-in-law did not end with the death of her parents-in-law. One of the most important aspects of filial piety was observation of the proper ancestor worship ceremonies. A filial son or daughter-in-law was he or she who expressed the most sorrow upon the parents' death and faithfully observed memorial services on the anniversary for three years. In mourning, the son and daughter-in-law were expected to show their devotion to the deceased parents in clearly visible forms that had symbolic meaning to others.

Naehun describes the rules succinctly:

> In mourning their parents, sons should live in a newly built hut, never remove mourning clothes made of cotton, sleep on a rough mat with a soil mound as a pillow, never untie a green belt, and never sit with other people.[38]

The daughter-in-law joined her husband in the mourning, and also took care of him during the period of mourning. Ancestor worship ceremony as an expression of the son's filial duty was the responsibility of the son in the formal sense, but the daughter-in-law in fact was in charge of carrying out the ceremony. It is interesting to note that one of the most important items in the education of girls before marriage was instruction in carrying out ancestor worship ceremony.

In reality, the death of her parents-in-law marked the end of the woman's following. In the last stage of the life cycle, she was supposed to follow her son, who was expected to be filial to her. This following was never to be enforced in the way the two previous forms were, as it will become clear in the next section.

Wise Mother, Mother-in-Law.

When a son married, a woman's following terminated, although the principle of three followings stipulated that she should follow her son. This rule was essentially incompatible with the rule of filial piety on the part of the son. In reality, the latter was more emphasized than the former. By this time, a woman must have mastered the principle of following. Confucian scholars and officials in the Chosun Dynasty tried to give positive value to the principle of following by stipulating the rule in the clearest possible manner, and by denying any possibility for women to resist this rule by creating other rules. Despite the enormous potentiality of tension within the family, the rules were that conflicts should not be manifested under any circumstances. Men's authority was balanced not by their responsibility but by women's following. The family order, sustained largely by women's following, required the development of enormous strength in women: such strength allowed them to endure all difficulties without dissent. This strength became the basis of the woman's existence, which helped support the order without ever overtly challenging it.

The most positive aspect of this existential strength of woman was represented in her as a wise mother. The meaning of the last rule, which stated that the woman should follow her son if her husband died, was never very clear. Given the premise that women should not have any will to be self-governing, the mother's following of her son may be interpreted as delegating to sons the authority and rights to make decisions on family matters. On the other hand, sons were supposed to be filial to their mothers, and hence the mother's authority was automatically recognized. In traditional Korea, unlike husband-wife relationships where the man leads and the woman follows, the mother-son relationship was one in which the relationship was built on mutual following. While the mother as a woman followed her son as a man, hierarchically the mother exercised authority over her son. In short, the mother following her son was offset by the son following the mother. And hence this relationship became the most harmonious one.

Furthermore, the rule of husband-wife distinction created a social distance between the two, arbitrary though it was, and in turn created the possibility for the mother to develop more affection for her son. The above rule also made child-rearing a prime duty of the mother, with the father remaining in the background. These considerations inevitably point to the mother-son relationship being characterized by the least conflict within the family setting. There is another factor contributing to the solidarity of mother and son. The custom which prohibited the remarriage of widows, although stemming from the principle of a woman serving only one man, in reality made the son-mother relationship a permanent one. While the mother was expected to think about her body originating from her parents, she also thought about the son as a part of her. The mother tended to project her own image onto her son. In traditional Korea a wise woman, in most cases, expressed herself through her son by asking him to be a model man, a filial son, a loyal subject, or otherwise distinguished in character. To use a modern expression, two selves merged almost perfectly. Chosun Dynasty Korea produced many wise mothers of famous men—loyal subjects, examplary statesmen, scholars, artists, and others—whose stories, together with that of Mencius' mother,[39] became immortalized in both intellectual traditions and folklore.

Paradoxical as it may sound, the filial piety rule was most successfully practiced in the mother-son relationship, approaching the ideal type conceived by Confucius.

The same woman, mother to her son, in the same family setting, turned into a mother-in-law to her daughter-in-law. The very word carried sinister meaning. Having gone through a period of hardship as a daughter-in-law, a woman reached the point where she no longer was in the position of following others but in a position of authority, if for no other than becoming a mother-in-law to a daughter-in-law. This shift from a subordinate position to a superordinate position was accompanied by a new expectation toward her daughter-in-law. She knew only too well that she could expect servitude from her daughter-in-law, as she has herself served her in-laws. Naturally, she wanted her daughter-in-law to repeat that. It has often been stated that the mother-in-law was too harsh from the point of view of the daughter-in-law, who cursed the position she was in. Apparently, women tended to develop an attitude of, "Since I have gone through it you should go through the same, otherwise it is not fair." Mothers-in-law were usually depicted as authoritarian in character, with little sympathy for others. Regardless of the status distinction, a mother-in-law was not likely to be a woman of understanding and affection. A local folk song described a young daughter-in-law's image of her new family:

> Tiger may be strong but could it be stronger than father-in-law?
> Chili sauce may be hot, but could it be hotter than mother-in-law?
> Peach flower may be pretty but could it be prettier than husband?[40]

A woman died as a wise mother as well as an unyielding mother-in-law, completing her life cycle. An epitaph written for an unknown woman by Lady Chonildang Kang summarizes the life of a woman in Chosun Dynasty Korea:

> Lady Yu was a sincere and docile woman. She lost her father when she was a child; she was most filial to her mother. She also took care of her brother and sister with love. After she married, she devoted herself fully to her parents-in-law, and treated her brother-in-law with sisterly affection. When her parents-in-law were most unhappy about her barrenness she accepted it calmly without showing any anger. She was even so diligent in weaving that kinsfolk rarely saw her blowing out the candle. She did cooking and sewing with utmost care to the point of being orderly.[41]

Alternatives.

While the social role of women in Confucian Korea was being structured and implemented with such intensity, numerous comments and criticisms by some Confucian scholars were levelled against the rigidity and inflexibility of the ideal women's role. These critiques did not, however, challenge directly the ideological basis of ethics pertaining to women, but rather extended sympathy to women for what they had to go through by virtue of their being women. Women themselves apparently accepted their situations as they were. Women were told and admitted that "they are life-long sinners." Fatalistic acceptance of women's position in Chosun Dynasty Korea was a common theme in what may be roughly translated as women's literature. Women lamented their hardships but never revolted against the society run by men. There is a sense in which the men's ideology of women turned into a theology for women. Women in Confucian Korea developed a form of existentialism based on the negation of existence, as a survival mechanism in a strictly authoritarian setting. They never expressed ideas denying the validity of Confucian ideology or sought to change it. Women only followed the narrowly defined women's way, and there was no other choice socially acceptable.

Women in Chosun Korea, especially those women born into *yangban* families, were expected to marry at a certain age, and without getting married they ceased to be full-fledged members of the society. There also was a law against remaining unmarried. *Sok Taechon* (Further Code of Law) says:

> Regarding those who passed the age of marriage -
> the government should hand out an order to provincial governments to look for them and help them to get married.[42]

Kyongkuk Taechon further elaborates the above rule:

> A daughter of *yangban* parents who remains single until the age of thirty due to financial difficulty, should make a request to the department of rites for financial aid.[43]

And it also stipulated that single persons should report to the same department every two years. Then it goes on to say:

> If a daughter of *yangban* parents remained single until the age of thirty for the reason of family poverty, the parents should be severely punished.[44]

It remains, of course, to be further assessed as to how effectively these laws regarding marriage were kept. But there clearly was a custom of early marriage, which was universally practiced. One can therefore infer that parents of *yangban* families were eager to have their daughter married at an appropriate age. The age of marriage was dictated by *Taechon Hwetong* (The Book of Royal Decrees), compiled in 1865, as follows:

> Men are allowed to marry at the age of 15, women at 14. If any of the parents of both families suffer from a chronic disease, or is beyond the age of 50, they can have their children marry after informing the proper administrative office.[45]

Upon marriage, a person was no longer considered an adolescent and was granted official recognition as an adult. Marriage was the only legitimate means of attaining adult status in traditional Korea.

While there was a strict rule imposed upon women with regard to compulsory marriage, there also were severe restrictions on women doing other work than that related to the family. There were of course numerous jobs carried out by women: entertainers, medicine women, court women, shamans, etc. But they were con-

sidered to be suitable only to women of low status. In most cases
women occupying these positions were expected to "entertain"
men, as well as perform their jobs. It was therefore unthinkable to
consider the above occupations as alternatives to marriage for
women of nobility and their families wishing to maintain status in
their society.

Why, then, were men so concerned with the social role of
women? Why did they feel it necessary to hold them in such a tight
rein? Presumably, men did not want to share any part of the world
they commanded, for to do so would be to enter into competition
with women. In Chosun Dynasty Korea, where agriculture was
considered the backbone of the country, farming itself was considered as work for commoners, not for *yangban* elites. The nobility could choose to become either civil servants or literati, reading
Confucian classics or writing poetry. Since being a member of the
literati was not really a job in the strictest sense of the term, career
choice for *yangban* elites was limited only to officialdom. From the
very early period of imperial Korea, there were too many applica-
tions for too few openings in the administration. It appears that
Confucian scholars were especially defensive about guarding their
domain from the intrusion of women. *Yangban* women were not
allowed to become scholars. Yi Ik had this to say:

> Learning is men's work. How could women read books when they should
> take care of their families and ancestors daily and throughout the seasons?
> Those women who were well versed with history, ancient as well as recent,
> and discussed ceremonies and etiquettes did not necessarily make use of it,
> and more often than not abused learning as we so frequently witnessed.[46]

Other scholars more or less echoed the same sentiment. Intelligent
women from the *yangban* class nevertheless learned Chinese
characters. Some of them wrote poetry, and kept the poems hidden
in a chest. The descendants of these women later collected the
poems, compiled them into books, and published them. Women's
intellectual activities took place only within the family setting, and
they never actively participated in the scholarly communities. Yun-
chidang Lady Yun distinguished herself with her remarkable intellectual maturity while she was young, which moved one of her
brothers so much that he once told his sister: "It is rather unfortunate that you, my sister, were not born as a man. You could have
become a great scholar."[47]

To summarize, the Confucian ideal of a virtuous woman was one who possessed the following qualities:

Woman's virtue: it is better to be calm and faithful than to be bright and clever;

Woman's language: it is better to avoid uttering bad words or words which would displease others than to be fluent;

Woman's countenance: it is better to be clean than to be pretty;

Woman's merit: it is better to be diligent than to be talented.

It appears that women became a perfect target for Confucian scholars and officials in their efforts to implant Confucian ethics, the practices of which would approximate the ideal types envisaged in the classics. Men were far more diligent in ensuring the conformity of women to the female ideal than they were about conforming to the model of the Confucian male. The rules of conduct tend to be more rigidly defined when they are not applied to the authors themselves.

Notes

1. The Confucian era refers to the period of Chosun Dynasty (1392-1910) in contradistinction to the previous dynasty, Koryo (918-1910) which was under heavey influence of Buddhism.
2. The Korean alphabet was invented by King Sechong (r. 1418-1450) but did not replace the Chinese script as the official language. Throughout the Chosun Dynasty period it was treated by Confucian scholars and officials as an undignified language only suitable for women to learn.
3. See Yi Neunghwa, *Chosun Yosongko* (Seoul: Daeyang Sochok, 1975), pp. 358-359.
4. Quoted by Park Yong-Ok, *Yi-Cho Yosongsa* (The History of Women in Chosun Dynasty Korea) (Seoul: Hankuk Ilbosa, 1976), p. 34.
5. Translated by Richard Rutt in his "The Chinese Learning and Pleasure of a Country Scholar," *Transactions* of Korea Branch of the Royal Asiatic Society, Vol. 34 (April, 1960), p. 92.
6. See Yi Neunghwa, *op. cit.,* p. 254.
7. See *Ibid.,* p. 252.
8. *Ye Ki,* or, Book of Rites, Volume 1, translated by James Legge (Hyde Park: University Books, 1967), p. 470.
9. Yi Neunghwa, *op. cit.,* p. 96.
10. Quoted by Yi Neugnhwa, *Ibid.,* p. 99.
11. One of the most frequently quoted passages from *Kongcha Ka'o* (The Selected Sayings of Confucius).
12. Yi Neunghwa, *op. cit.,* p. 329.
13. *Hyokyong* or *Hsia Ching* (Classic of Filial Piety), translated into Korean by Yi Minsu (Seoul: Eulyu Moonhwasa, 1971), p. 25.

14. *Ibid.*, p. 26.

15. *Ibid.*, p. 72.

16. See Yi Neunghwa, *op. cit.*, (pp. 329-256), and Kim Kyung-Jin, "Chosun Wang-cho sillok'e kichedwen hyonyo, cholpu'e kwanhan soko - Taechong Sillok - Chungchong Sillok'ul chungsim'euro," (A Study of Filial Daughters and Chaste Women as Recorded in Chosun Dynasty Royal *Veritable Records* - with Special Reference to *Taechong-Chungchong Sillok, Asea Yosong Yonku* (Journal of Asian Women), Vol. 16 (1977), pp. 47-72.

17. *Ibid.*

18. *Op. cit.*

19. Yi Neunghwa, *op. cit.*

20. Yi Sok-nae, *Yicho ui Yoinsang* (The Image of Women in Yi Dynasty Korea) (Seoul: Eulyu Moonhwasa, 1973), pp. 104-108.

21. See Kim Yong-sook, "Ko-sosok'e natanan aechongkwan" (Views on Affection in Pre-Modern Novels) *Asea Yosong Yonku* (Journal of Asian Women) Vol. 13 (1974), pp. 47-76.

22. Ho Nansolhon and others, *Yokdae Yoryu Hansimunson* (A Selection of Poems and Essays in Chinese by Women Writers in Chosun Dynasty Korea), translated by Kim Chi-Yong (Seoul: Daeyang Sochok, 1975), p. 317.

23. A popular expression widely used by Confucian scholars describing themselves.

24. Hong Daeyong, *Damhonso* (Collected Essays by Damhon), translated by Chon Kwanwoo and Yu Seungchoo (Seoul: Daeyang Sochok, 1975), p. 79.

25. *Daejae Yeki* (Book of Rites of the Elder Tae) (Circa 1st century B.C.).

26. See Yim Dong-Kwon, "Chop kwa chongsang'ui kwanhan buyu (Folksongs on Concubines and Young Widows)", *Asea Yosong Yonku* (Journal of Asian Women), Vol. 5 (1966), pp. 117-148.

27. *Ibid.*, p. 34.

28. Park Yong-Ok, *op. cit.*, p. 114.

29. Quoted by Park Yong-Ok, *op. cit.*, p. 123. On the historical debates on widow remarriage, see also Lee Sang-Beck, *Hanukuk Munhwasa Yonku Nonko* (A Study on Korean Cultural History) (Seoul: Eulyu Moonhwasa, 1949), pp. 205-248.

30. Quoted by Yi Neunghwa, *op. cit.*, p. 169.

31. Quoted by Yi Neunghwa, *op. cit.*, p. 171.

32. *Ibid.*, p. 172.

33. *Ibid.*, p. 174.

34. *Ibid.*, p. 177.

35. Park, *op. cit.*, p. 115.

36. See Kim Chi-Yong, "Naehun'e bichuochin Yicho yoindeul'ui saeng-hwalsang" (Life of the Woman in Yi Dynasty Korea as Reflected in Naehun) *Asea Yosong Yonku* (Journal of Asian Women), Vol. 7, 1968, p. 189.

37. *Ibid.*, p. 189.

38. *Ibid.*, p. 191.

39. Mencius' mother moved three times when he was a child, each time because she thought the surroundings were not congenial to her son's education.

40. See Yim Dong-Kwon, "Sijipsali-Yo Ko" (A Study of Folksongs on Daughters-in Law) *Asea Yosong Yonku* (Journal of Asian Women), Vol. 2 (1963), pp. 25-78.

41. Ho Nansolhon, *op. cit.,* pp. 348-349.

42. Quoted by Yi Neunghwa, *op. cit.,* p. 148.

43. Quoted by Yi Neunghwa, *ibid.,* p. 135.

44. Quoted by Yi Neunghwa, *ibid.,* p. 135.

45. Quoted by Yi Neunghwa, *ibid.,* p. 147.

46. Quoted by Ha Hyon-kang, "Chosun Sidae" (The Chosun Period) in Hankuk Yosongsa Pyonchan Wiwonhoe (The Committee on Compilation of the History of Women in Korea), *Hankuk Yosongsa* (The History of Women in Korea), (Seoul: Ewha Women's University Press, 1972), p. 572.

47. Quoted by Park Yong-Ok, *op. cit.,* p. 169.

Acknowledgment

I am grateful to Michael Kew for his critical comments and editorial assistance. My appreciation also goes to the Social Sciences and Humanities Research Council of Canada (formerly the Canada Council) for financial support of my project on Shamanistic practices in Korea, from which this paper resulted.

6 / Kagok: The Music for Yi Intellectuals

BYONG-KON KIM

Kagok was the most important form of Korean vocal music enjoyed by the scholars of the Yi Dynasty (1392-1910) and, possibly, of the preceding second half of the Koryo Dynasty. The scholars of the periods were also politicians, philosophers and poets. *Kagok* was in the center of the entertainment for seasonal *fêng-liu* (風流) poetry meetings, such as Spring Flower and Willow, Summer Breeze, Autumn Full-moon, Winter Snow-scene and others, which might be followed by extemporization of a poem by each participant. *Kagok* was never taught at the Royal Institute of Music for use in the Yi Court. Occasionally, however, *kagok* singers were called upon to perform in the palace.

Nineteen movements of a *kagok,* sometimes called *Man-yon-chang-whan-ji-gok* (Eternal Pleasure Music), can be sung by a male soloist, or by a group of female singers in unison, or alternated by a male singer and a group of female singers. This long suite, which may take several hours, was accompanied by a chamber ensemble consisting of a single *komungo, ka ya gum, yanggum, saep'iri, tae gum, tanso, haegum* and *changgo.*

Kagok was categorized as *chong-song* (正声),[1] righteous or orthodox vocal music, the counterpart of which was *sori, song.*[2]
The former tends to be more dignified, objective, serene and optimistic, while the latter can be described as more vigorous, theatrical, pathetic, descriptive, and subjective.

Philosophical Background

Until the eighteenth century *kagok* was not only patronized solely by scholars but also was created by their participation in poetry. Chinese philosophies and Buddhism were introduced to Korea during a much earlier time than the period described in this study. Chinese philosophy, Confucianism in particular, and Buddhism, were directly or indirectly involved in Korean politics for many centuries. Confucianism especially cast the mold of Korean politics and ethics during the last nine hundred years. In this period, if a man was educated at all, the first education he received was philosophy. Philosophy was the concern of every educated person.

Confucius did not mention the aesthetics of music, but, in general, his view was, like Plato, that music is an ideal instrument in ethical and political education. In the *Confucian Analects* (Book IV, Chapter 8),

> The Master said that education starts with poetry, flourishes in ritual (*Li*) and accomplishes in music.

Also, in the *Analects* (Book 8, Chapter 15), we find:

> Answering to Yen Yuan's question on the principles in ruling a state, the Master said to use the calendar of Hsia, ride a carriage of Yin, follow the bureaucratic system of Chou, and dance to Shao music of Shun. Since the music of Ch'eng is obscene and eloquent persons are not trustworthy, avoid music of Ch'eng and eloquent persons.

Further, the *Book of Music, Yueh-chi* (樂記), of the *Li-chi* (禮記), *Book of Ritual,* which is one of the Six Classics that every learned man has to know, says that,

> Sound is born by the mind. Music communicates with ethics. . . .
> . . . Only a man of complete virtue understands music. Experiencing sound he understands music. Experiencing music he understands politics. Thus, the Golden Rule of administering a state is accomplished. . . One who attained *Li* and *Yüeh* (樂) [music] is called benevolent. . .

Away from a purely educational function of music the teachings of Confucius drew guidelines as to what and how music should be. He stated in his *Treatise on Music,* (*Yüeh-chi* 樂記), (Chapter 20) that ,

> Man cannot be without joy, and when there is joy, it must have a physical embodiment. When this embodiment does not conform to the right principle, there will be disorder. The early kings hated this disorder, and so they established the music of the *Ya* 雅 and *Sung* 頌 to guide it. They caused its music to be joyful and not degenerate, and its beauty to be distinct and not limited. They caused it in its indirect and direct appeals, its complexity and simplicity, its

frugality and richness, its rests and notes, to stir up the goodness in man's minds and to prevent evil feelings from gaining any foothold. This is the manner in which the early kings established music.[3]

Confucius expressed his pleasure with the music of Kwan-sui (關雎) by stating in the Analects (Book 2, Chapter 3): "It is pleasant yet not obscene, mournful yet not distressing." Views on a similar subject are found in the Samguk Sagi which states:[4]

> The Tae-ak (大樂) (Great Music) of Silla was pleasant yet not vulgar, mournful yet not pathetic.

In the same book, it is recorded that the Silla musician U-Ruk's nine musical compositions were inherited by his pupils. But four of these were eliminated because they were "busy and unstable, busy and sensuous" (繁且慢繁且淫). However, none was more positive toward music than the statement in the Book of Music, (Yüeh-chi) [樂記], of the Li-chi (禮記), "music is in what a sage takes pleasure."[5]

Taoists, who saw the world merely as a phenomenon born out of natural law and man as an observer who only reflects it in his mind and who tries to escape from it to preserve purity, had no formal treatise on art. Their idealization of nature, however, inspired many artists for generations to come, e.g., huao-niao-fêng-yüeh (花鳥風月), flower-bird-scenery-and-moon, was the favorite subject of arts until the end of the eighteenth century in China as well as in neighboring countries. Unlike Confucianism, which had positive views toward politics and the world, Taoism did not become the main philosophy among scholars. However, a shade of Taoism was always felt in Korean society.

Neo-Confucianism was developed by the Ch'eng brothers[6] and Chu Hsi (1130-1200), in China, with some influence from the philosophies of Taoism and Buddhism. Chu Hsi explains in Chu-Tzu-Chûan-Shu, Vol 49 that T'ai-Chi, the Supreme Ultimate,[7] is "like, within us, a pearl in turbid water." This obscurity is made by Ch'ing (情), selfish desire. The first step of cultivation for restoration of the Supreme Ultimate is by advancement of learning, which is not limited to the study of the classics but also attainment of Tao and the truth. Extension of one's knowledge is emphasized. The next step is to disconnect oneself from Ch'ing and ensnarement. If one reaches the point where he is free from *Ch'ing,* and without effort, he can be impersonal and impartial to things and respond to things spontaneously as they come; he can be considered a sage, which would bring unmatched satisfaction. Such a search for happiness had been outlined variously by many Confucianists since Men Tzu. To Chou Tung-Yi, it was vacuous quiescence and straightforwardness in movement. To Ch'eng Hao, it was to enjoy what he himself was, i.e., to be natural himself without *Ch'ing.* Also *fêng-liu* (風流), poetical life with nature, was considered to be the most desirable for a scholar. On the other hand, however, Neo-Confucianists did not negate the existence of emotion. The sage's mind is, like a mirror, impartial and objective. It will simply reflect as an objective phenomenon whatever state of emotion comes to him.

Although some of these philosophies meet the criteria of religion, acceptance of them as learning rather than religion have created a far greater impact on the culture of China and Korea. Accordingly, the spiritual and magical power of music that was believed by Western scholars of music-aesthetics to exist during the Middle Ages was hardly recognized in the music of *Kagok.*

Not many direct citations of Neo-Confucian philosophy on music in Korea can be cited. However, straightforward adoption of musical literature in Chu Hsi's *Ilich'ingch'uan T'ungchiai Shiyûeh* (儀禮經傳通解詩樂) by the Yi Court in 1430 A.D. for Royal Morning Reception Music is one of the evidences of direct influence of Neo-Confucianism.[8]

The Confucian moralistic and philosophical view of music watched, guided and cultivated the type of music that was enjoyed by scholars. An instrumental music in this category is, typically, *chong-ak* (正樂), righteous and straightforward music; the vocal music is *chong-song* (正聲), righteous and straightforward vocal music. Philosophies of *chong-ak* and *chong-song* may be summarized: beauty should be distinct and not limited; it should stir up goodness in man's mind and prevents evil feelings; it should be neither busy nor sensuous, but stable; it should be nature-loving and free from selfish desire; impersonal, impartial and spontaneous; it should be of vacuous quiescence and strightforward, reflecting emotion but not distressing or pathetic. This was the music for a scholar, a supreme man or sage.

The music that did not meet this outline was considered vulgar and undesirable and not fitting for scholars. If this type of music was found in cultured society it was to be purged, as it was on several occasions during the Yi Dynasty. In 1430 A.D. Pak Yon, director of the Office of Royal Music, petitioned "to declare that music on ethical subjects be the Correct Music and that on obscene, carnal and shameful subjects be Detestable Music."[9] In 1488 A.D., Yi Saezwa petitioned to abolish the following three musical compositions from the Royal Music Repertoire on the basis of their being fleshly and vulgar:[10] *Hu-jong-wha, Man-jon-ch'un,* and *Sa-gun-ga.* All had been performed frequently in the Royal Court. Also, King Song-jong (reigned 1470-1494) eliminated *Ssang-wha-jom,* which had been played in the court often, saying that "this is a tune of fleshly pleasure. I have no choice but to abandon it."[11] One of the two culminating Neo-Confucianists in Korea, Yi Whang, deplored intellectuals' indulgence in obscene music. Hoping to establish models of poetry for a learned man, he published his twelve poems in 1565 A.D.[12]

On the other hand, two compositions were added to the Royal music repertoire during King Song-jong's period. *Chong-gwa-jong,* a song of loyalty by Chong-gwa-jong himself, was adopted as a standard composition that every royal musician was tested with. The other was *Kyonggi-ch'aegas,* a number of poems of music written by Koryo loyalists, that flourished at scholars' salons until the middle of the Yi period and included in the repertoire of Royal Court Music.

Sijo and The Evolution of Kagok

A lyrical poem, *sijo* was written and enjoyed by scholars and was the most important form of poetry in Yi Korea. *Sijo* is believed to have been written for *kagok* from the beginning. The Chinese character *si* (時) is for "time" or "current," and *jo* (調) is for "tune" or "rhyme." The name *sijo* was not used until the early eighteenth century when the singer-poet Yi Sae-ch'un used the term for the poetic genre. The name *tanga* (短歌), [short poem], was used for these poems until that time. However, the originality of the term *sijo* is disputable.[13]

Sijo poetry can be divided into two categories according to

construction: *P'yong-sijo* (平時調) and *chang-sijo*
(長時調).*P'yong-sijo* has three lines to a stanza with each line
consisting of four poetic feet, for a total of twelve poetic feet. The
number of syllables to each poetic foot is usually:

> First line: 3, 4, 4, 4 or 3
> Second line: 3, 4, 4, 4 or 3
> Third line: 3, 5, 4, 3

However, the number of syllables in each poetic foot varies
considerably, except the ninth poetic foot. Since the accent on the
first syllable of a word or poetic foot in the Korean language is
crucial, the variance of the number of syllables in a poetic foot does
not alter the format of the poem. A poetic foot, a group of syllables
with an accent usually on the initial syllable, is normally constructed of either three or four syllables in Korean poetry. Yang
Yom-kyu defines the three-syllable foot as being derived from the
Korean folk song tradition and the four-syllable foot to be from
Hyangga tradition.[14] An example of poetic meter found in a
pyong-sijo, Imomi chukgo chuko, reveals its musical implication.

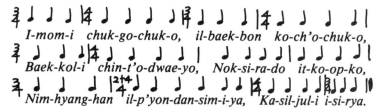

I-mom-i chuk-go-chuk-o, il-baek-bon ko-ch'o-chuk-o,
Baek-kol-i chin-t'o-dwae-yo, Nok-si-ra-do it-ko-op-ko,
Nim-hyang-han il-p'yon-dan-sim-i-ya, Ka-sil-jul-i i-si-rya.

Chang-sijo, which evolved during the middle of the seventeenth century, can be further divided into two categories, *Ot-sijo*
and *Sasol-sijo. Ot-sijo* is a *sijo* with more than four poetic feet in
the first and the second lines, while *sasol-sijo* has more than four
poetic feet in all three lines.

The origin of *sijo* is not fully known. Though the oldest extant
sijo, [15] *tanka,* is by Ch'wae Ch'ung (d. 1068) of the early period of
Koryo, it was toward the end of the Koryo Dynasty that *sijo* was
established and flourished. The poetry was evolved exclusively by
the Neo-Confucianists. A summary of *Shih-Ch'ing* (詩經) in
the *Confucian Analects* (Book 8, Chapter 2) says that ''the essence

of them can be covered in one sentence: Have not depraved thoughts.'' (思 無 邪   ). This must have contributed to the climate of the *sijo* evolution. Escaping from the common daily subjects and amiable topics of poetry of the time, the Neo-Confucianists succeeded in creating poetry that was based on Confucian ethics and ideals.

Neo-Confucianism was introduced to Koryo around 1300 A.D. by either An Yu (安 裕) or Paek Yi-jong (白頤正). Accelerated by the adoptation of *Kwa-go,* governmental examination for the selection of officials tested knowledge of Confucian teaching and Confucian philosophy prevailed throughout the country toward the last period of the Koryo Dynasty. Ch'wae U's military government (1214-1259) resulted in a mass exodus of Neo-Confucianists into the mountains seeking a quiet life away from the hustle of the world. Ironically, this was what Neo-Confucianist philosophy could very well accept. Topics often dealt with the moon, flowers, snow, bamboo, or other such nature-oriented themes. The examination of nature became acceptable if not ideal in Neo-Confucianism, becoming the way of life in the following seven hundred years for scholars when they met Royal disfavor. However, it should be noted that there was a difference between Taoistic escapism and practical Neo-Confucianistic retirement into nature waiting for the King's favor again. For the same reason, there were a great number of poems on royalty, and panegyric themes. With the establishment of the new Yi dynasty in 1392, the fundamental Confucian value and order reached every spectrum of society.

Unlike the classifications of Korean history usually used by historians, this study will follow the author's own classifiations for the convenience of discussion of *kagok.* The first period is from 1392 to 1592, the year of the Hideyoshi Invasion. The second period extends to 1725, covering the wars with Japan and China, and partisan wrangling. The third period, up to 1800, often called the *Yong-chong* Period, represents reconstruction and Practical Learning. The period up to 1910, the fourth, witnessed the decline of the empire.

Civil governance was seen during the first period of the Yi Dynasty, which also witnessed the culmination of the study and practice of Neo-Confucianism.[16] *Hangul,* the Korean alphabet, which made *sijo* a truly indigenous poetry, was invented and put to use in 1446. Until then, poems were translated into Chinese characters or *yi-du,* Chinese characters used to represent sound without meaning, and were later retranslated into the new alphabet, *hangul.*

Numerous *sijo,* (*p'yong-sijo* exclusively) were written by a great number of poet-scholars during this period. Topics ranged widely, but the most frequently used subjects were the beauty of nature; the satisfaction of living in nature; Taoistic escapism; didactic themes of self-cultivation; loyalty to king, country and party, and friendship. *P'yong-sijo* reached its culmination during this period.

Due to the small number of extant musical manuscripts from the period, it is rather difficult to reconstruct a complete picture of the state of *kagok.* The oldest extant music is found in *Kum Hapja-bo,*[17] (*Anthology of Komungo Music*), written by An Sang and published in 1572. It includes only *Man-dae-yop* (慢大葉), which is a *kagok* in an extremely slow tempo. Also, *Taeak, Hubo*[18] an anthology of King Saejo's court music covering the years 1456-1470, recorded *Man-dae-yop* only. The aesthetic value of *Man-dae-yop* to scholars of the first period can be detected in a letter of Yi Tokyun to Chong Tuwon and the latter's reply:[19]

> *Man-dae-yop* is the ancestor of all other *kagok* repertoire. For its quiescence, naturalness, and plainness, if it is performed by an enlightened person, the music is reminiscent of smoothness of spring cloud floating in the air, of vastness of fragrant breeze sweeping over a plain. Also, it sounds as if thousands of dragons flirting in water, and a crane singing on a pine tree. There is a clear distinction from music that would cause disorder in the country. . .

In reply, Chong Tuwon said:[20]

> The content of your letter is most appreciatively concurred. My humble opinion is that *Man-dae-yop* is slow yet not despair [sic]. Therefore, the country may experience temporary disorder but will never decline. . .

The second period of the Yi Dynasty (1591-1725) was the period of internal and external turmoil. The Hideyoshi invasion was followed by a Chinese invasion and continuous party wrangling. This was the "dark age" in the history of the Yi Dynasty. The loss of grip by the central government, disappointment in

metaphysical learnings of scholars, caused by the tragedies of party
fighting and economic drain, brought about interest in the Practical Learnings, and yearning for peace and prosperity in daily life.
The total monopoly of *kagok* by rather aristocratic scholars was
broken. Especially toward the end of the period, participation of
the common people in writing *sijo* and other cultural activity was
greatly increased.

Numerous *sijo* on the theme of loyalty to the nation and the
King were still written during the earlier part of the second period.
But *chang-sijo* took hold of the ground rapidly. *Chan-sijo* eventually became a very popular poetry form. Along with the participation of the common people in writing, the old themes of bamboo, clouds, and the Taoism of *p'yong-sijo* gradually made way for
more chattier and informal *chang-sijo* to deal with the subject of
daily life, love, emotion, humor and banal events. These *chang-sijo*
often use a vocabulary of common speech and conversation in
realistic and descriptive manner. The moralistic grip of the previous
period was lessened, even in *p'yong-sijo*.

This popular patronage of *kagok* invited a number of anthologies to be written. Only the musical repertoire from the
previous period *man-dae-yop* was retained but two new repertoires
were added: one was *chung-dae-yop*, music of a medium tempo
while the other was *sak-dae-yop*, music of a fast tempo. In the
Yanggum Sinbo (梁琴新譜), *Yang's Komungo Anthology*, of
1610, by Yang Toksu, appeared *man-dae-yop* and *chung-dae-yop*.
Sak-dae-yop is mentioned as a dance music but the music itself is
not included. *Hyongum Tongmun Yugi* (玄琴東文類記),
of 1620, by Yi Tukyun included *man-dae-yop, chung-dae-yop* and
sak-dae-yop. *Paekunam Kumbo* (白雲庵琴譜)[21] by an
unknown author, but believed to be compiled between 1610 and
1680, [22] included all three *dae-yops*. Also, in the two anthologies by
Sin Song, compiled in 1680, *Hyongum Sinjong Karyong*
(玄琴新證假令), and *Sin-song Kumbo* (申晟琴譜), appeared all three *dae-yops*.

However, another anthology which was compiled almost a
half century later by Kim Ch'unt'aek reveals a remarkable evolution that had taken place. Kim Ch'unt'aek's *Ch'onggu Yongon*
(靑丘永言). was compiled in 1727. This is an anthology of current
sijo poems classified according to the types of music used in *kagok*.

Here, *man-dae-yop* was not included although it included
numerous *chung-dae-yop* and *sak-dae-yop*. *Man-dae-yop* had apparently lost the people's favor during the period between 1680 and
1727. Later, Yi Yik (李瀷) (1682-1764) wrote in his book
Songho Sasol (星湖僿説), of unknown date, the fate of
man-dae-yop:

> *Man-dae-yop* was disliked by people because it was too slow. *Chung-dae-
> yop* was the same. Presently, only *sak-dae-yop* remains to be performed.[23]

In addition to a number of *chung-dae-yop* and *sak-dae-yop*,
however, *Ch'onggu Yongon* included *so-yung* (騒聳); *onrong*
(言弄); *rong* (弄); *onrak* (言樂); *p'yonrak* (編樂), and
p'yon-su-dae-yop (編數大葉).

The reigns of King Yóngjo and King Chongjo, during the third
period, is considered the golden age of *kagok*. Study in the Practical Learning was greatly promoted and art reached down to the
middle or lower-middle class of society. The majority of poets of
the time were lower level officials, *kisaengs,* housewives as well as
scholars. The weariness of the wars disappeared and this was
reflected in daily life as well as in cultural activities. More than in
the previous period, poetry and music became peoples' arts.

Chang-sijo blossomed in the third period. New music for
chang-sijo introduced during the past period was expanded and
became a major body in the *kagok* repertoire. It can be said that
kagok also reached its peak in terms of size, variety, and ac-
cessibility—although not necessarily in quality. It should be noted
that the mutation of *kagok* took place due to the change of
aesthetics on the part of patrons and artists. Other anthologies
completed during the period confirm the similar line of music
literatures as found in *Ch'onggu Yongon.*[24]

This, also, was the time when a great singer, Yi Saech'un, initiated a new genre of music using the *sijo* poem called *sijo-ch'ang*
(時調唱). Unlike *kagok, sijo-ch'ang,* which means "*sijo* singing," is performed as individual pieces rather than a suite. The
duration of each *sijo-ch'ang* is shorter and shows a lesser structural
expansion while the accompaniment is reduced to a *changgo* or to
nothing. The *sijo-ch'ang* became a favorite genre of music of the
people.

The fourth period, after about 1800, marks the decline of the

Yi Dynasty and the modernization of the country; the *sijo* genre and poetry also declined in number and quality. However, *kagok* not only sustained its momentum but also added new music and was performed fairly often. *Kagok Wonryu* (歌曲源流), by Pak Hyogwan and An Minyong, (1876), still included *chung-dae-yop*. Otherwise the repertoire in the book is almost the same as that of the twentieth century version. *Hyongum Oum T'ongron* (玄琴五音統論), that appeared in 1886, by Yun Yonggu, is the earliest anthology that does not include *chung-dae-yop*. It can be assumed that the shift was gradual although the direction was definite. In the twentieth century, when most circumstances do not fit the performance of an entire suite, traditional musicians say that only one or two faster compositions are usually played "because the slow pieces are boring." Most of the present-day repertorie, in faster tempo, was developed to replace the old. This shift coincided with a shift of philosophy—the de-emphasis of Neo-Confucianism and a shift to Practical Learnings; change of patronage from *p'yong-sijo* to *chang-sijo,* and a change from scholar-aristocrats to the common people.

P'yong-sijo on nature, Taoism, loyalty, friendship and self-cultivation became low key, and the stage for the hero of Korean poetry yielded to the new *chang-sijo* from the second period. Solemn, unpretentious, unsophiscated and detached, *p'yong-sijo* became secondary to more descriptive, grandiloquent, and hedonistic *chang-sijo*. *Chang-sijo* dealt with the subjects of daily life—love, emotion, wine, humor, peace and pleasure, jokes, and even obscenity. However, *chang-sijo,* along with the mood of westernization, lost its charm and identity with the people toward the end of the nineteenth century.

The *Anthology of Korean Traditional Music*[25] includes eighty *p'yong-sijo* and seventy-six *chang-sijo* that are currently used in *kagok*. This is the literature that can be more likely heard at the present and is the largest collection of this sort. The following tables are the result of a statistical analysis of the themes of *kagok*. Loyalty, panegyrics, Taoistic, didactic matters are more often in the *p'yong-sijo* form and sung by a male singer, while such subjects as *feng-liu* (peace and pleasure-seeking matters) are more often in the *chang-sijo* form and sung by female singers. Of the 156 *sijo* the authors of only twenty-four works are known, and those are exclusively of *p'yong-sijo*.[26]

Theme of poem

Movement & Performance order	Singer (M/P)	Scale	Total	Type of slose P. & C.	Loyalty, Panegyric	Nature, Theistic	Didactic	Pung-liu	Love, Longing	Sad-ness	Loyalty-soldier	Peace, Pleasure-seeking	Histori-cal	Hŭm-(Hŭm?)	Others & Unclassi-fyable
1. Ch'odu-dae-yŏp	M	U	5	P	2	1	1		1						
2. I-su-dae yŏp	M P	M D	6 5	P P	1 1	2 1 1			1 2			1			1 2
3. Chung-gŏ	P	M D	6 5	P P		1 1	1		1 1	1					
4. P'yŏng-gŏ	M P	M D	5 5	P P	1	1 1			1 1			1 1			
5. Tu-gŏ	M P	M D	7 5	P P	2	2 2		1	1 1	1					
6. Sam-su-dae-yŏp	M	M	5	P&C	1	2 2		1(C)	1		1 1	1		3	1
7. So-yong-i	M	D	5	C					1			2			
8. Ŏn-rong	M	K	5	C		1		2 1	2	2					
9. P'yŏng-rong	M	U-M	5	C			1	1							
10. Pan-yŏp	P	U-K	10	C				1							
11. Ke-rak	M	M-K	6	C	2	1 1 2		3	2	1		1			1
12. U-rak	M P	D	7 3	C C				1 2	2						1 3
13. Ŏn-rak	M	U	6	C			2	1	2	2		2	1		2
14. P'yŏn-rak	M	U-M	3	C					1	1					
15. P'yŏn-u-dae-yŏp	P	K	9 7	C C				1 1	1 4 1				1		2 1
16. Ŏn-p'yŏn	M	K	2	C					1						
17. U-rong	M	U	1	C		1									
18. U-p'yŏn	M	D	2	C											
19. Whan-gye-rak	P	U-K	2	C									1	2	
20. T'ae-p'yŏng-ga	MP	K	1	P	1					1		1			1
21. Kae-rong	P	K	5	C					2				1		1
Total number of P and C	P C				9 2	23 6	3 3	2 15	26 15	5 4	2 0	3 7	0 1	0 5	0 16
Primarily sang by: (male or female)					M	M	M	M	P	P	M	M	P	M	M

Note: • "U" is for Ujo scale used in the music. "P" is for ...
• Primarily sang by: (male or female)

The names of poets and the themes they deal with in their *sijo* are:

POET	THEME
Yi Zono (1341-1371)	Loyalty
Yi Ch'onyon (1269-1343)	Love
King T'aejong (1367-1422)	Nature
Kim Chongso (1390-1453)	Loyalty-soldier
Pak P'aengnyon (1417-1456)	Loyalty
King Songjong (1457-1494)	King's love of subject
Whang Jini (c. 1506-1544)	Love
Ch'on Kum (16th C.)	Nature
Chong Sul (Late 16th C.)	Loyalty
So Ik (Late 16th C.)	Loyalty
Chong Ch'ol (1537-1594)	Nature
Sin Hum (1566-1628)	Nature
Kim Sanghon (1570-1652)	Righteousness
Yi Myonghan (1595-1645)	Love, Aging, Nature
King Hyojong (1619-1659)	Loyalty
Song Siyol (1607-1689)	Nature
Nam Kuman (1629-1711)	Nature
Chu Uisik (1675-1720)	Historic
An Minyong (c.1870)	Nature
Pak Hyogwan (fl. 1850)	Love

Two are from the Koryo period, nine are from the first period, seven from the second period, and two from the later periods of the Yi Dynasty. Even though this covers only a part of the eighty *p'yong-sijo*, it should be noted that *sijos* from the Koryo and the first period of the Yi Dynasty are still in use. It is true that *Kagok* of *chang-sijo*, other than the above, might be performed more often at the present time when short performance are required. However, it is again true that *kagok* movements on *p'yong-sijo*, *sak-dae-yop* and others, are claimed to be more authentic.

Music

There are twenty-six movements for a male singer and fifteen for a female in the entire repertoire of *kagok*.[27] Performances can be executed solely by male or female singers or alternated between the two.

Extremely meristematic *kagok* shows that the *p'yong-sijo* poem is divided into five sections, called chapters. The first two poetic feet are the first chapter and the following two feet become the second. The second line, which is the fifth through the eighth foot, represents the third chapter. The ninth foot alone makes the fourth chapter and the remainder is called the fifth chapter.

An interlude by the accompanying chamber group is placed at the end of the third chapter. The postlude is heard at the end of a movement. The postlude serves as prelude to the following movement except in the opening movement of the suite, which is *ch'o-su-dae-yop* in *kaemyon* or *u* mode, where *tasurim* is used for prelude. In preludes, interludes and postludes as well as accompaniment, each member of the chamber group plays a heterophonic line. The result is a quasi-contrapuntal texture. The *sae-piri* traces the vocal line with some degree of elaboration.

The *changgo* (drum) repeats a talea-like rhythmic pattern of sixteen beats, except several of ten beats,[28] throughout the movement. The following basic rhythmic pattern shows the metric subdivisions:

Right had (stick):
Left hand (drum head):

The ten-beat pattern is derived from the above pattern by eliminating one resting beat, a quarter rest, in each measure. *Tempi* of movements range from ♩ = 20 to ♩ = 80.

The slow *tempi* of *kagok,* where pulsation in most movements is hardly felt, along with a great degree of lineacy of the accompanying instruments, changing meters and an extreme melisma of vocal line, all combine to achieve a floating effect. Beside having some limitation on creating tension by means of dynamic volume in such a chamber ensemble, uniform attempts to make *crescendo* or *decrescendo* (or any variation of dynamic range) do not exist in the performance. Polyphony is not the best type of texture for frequently changing expression; it is more effective for a consistent ex-

pression during a longer span of time, and less descriptive, if not
abstract. A repeated simple rhythmic pattern, such as one with sixteen beats that takes twelve to forty-eight seconds, is not the best
material for expressive musical communication. Rather, it provides
a minimum function of keeping time without creating a regular
metric accent. Thus, expressive means such as building up tension
to a point and decreasing from it is not possible with such *tempi,*
rhythmic practice and the texture in *kagok.* On the other hand,
these are effectively used to create a more detached, less descriptive
music.

The following table is the repertoire and performance order
for a mixed voice version, and other movements that appear in
Lee's *Kagokbo* but not included in his suggested performance
order.

Order	Male-Female	Mode	Title of Movement	Tempo	Rhyth-mic Pattern	Type of Sijo Used
1	M	U	*Ch'o-su-dae-yop*	Medium	16	P
2	F	U	*I-su-dae-yop*	Slow	16	P
3	M	U	*Sam-su-dae-yop*	Medium	16	P
4	F	U	*Tu-go*	Medium	16	P
5	M	U	*So-yung-i*	Medium	16	C
6	F	U-K	*Pan-yop*	Fast-slow	16	P
7	M	K	*Ch'o-su-dae-yop*	Medium	16	P
8	F	K	*I-su-dae-yop*	Slow	16	P
9	M	K	*Sam-su-dae-yop*	Medium	16	P
10	F	K	*Tu-go*	Medium	16	P
11	M	K	*On-rong*	Medium	16	C
12	F	K	*P'yong-rong*	Medium	16	C
13	M	K	*Kae-rak*	Medium	16	P
14	F	K	*Kae-rak*	Medium	16	P
15	M	U	*On-rak*	Medium	16	C
16	F	U	*U-rak*	Medium	16	C
17	M	U-K	*P'yon-rak*	Fast-Med.	10	C
18	F	K	*P'yon-su-dae-yop*	Fast	10	C
19	M&F	K	*T'ae-p'yong-ga*	Medium	16	P

Male-Female	Mode	Title of Movement	Tempo	Rhythmic Pattern	Type of Sijo Used
Other movements not included in the suggested performance order are:					
M	U	*Chung-go*	Slow	16	P
M	K	*Chung-go*	Slow	16	P
F	U	*Chung-go*	Slow	16	P
F	K	*Chung-go*	Medium	16	P
M	U	*P'yong-go*	Medium	16	P
M	K	*P'yong-go*	Medium	16	P
F	U	*P'yong-go*	Medium	16	P
F	K	*P'yong-go*	Medium	16	P
M	U	*U-rong*	Medium	16	P
M	U	*U-p'yon*	Fast	10	C
M	K	*So-yung-i*	Medium	16	C
M	K	*P'yon-su-dae-yop*	Fast	10	C
M	K	*On-p'yon*	Fast	10	C
M	U-K	*Pan-yop*	Fast	16	P
F	U-K	*Whan-gae-rak*	Fast	16	C

NOTE: In mode, *U* is *U-jo*, *K* is for *Kae-myon-jo.* In tempo, "slow" is ♩ = 20-35, "medium" is ♩ = 40-55, "fast" is ♩ = 70-80 according to Lee Chuwhan in *Kagokbo-Sok* (歌曲譜續) (Seoul: Kukrib Kukakwon, 1962).

Interestingly enough, the recognition of composers in traditional music was uncommon. The authorship of poetry may be recorded, but not that of musical compositions. Usually, upon the completion of a poem, it was given to musicians to set to music. If the music was good enough to be accepted the composer's name was kept by oral tradition and not recorded. This process of acceptance or rejection was done by the audience of scholars.

Currently, two modes, *ujo* and *kaemyonjo,* are used in *kagok* and there are several movements starting in *ujo* that modulate to *kaemyonjo.* (See the preceding table). Analysis of the pitch spectrum of movements in *ujo* shows that B-flat; C, E-flat, F and A-flat are basic pitches of the mode. The vocal melodic cadence is always on F except in one case which is on B-flat the cadence of the postlude is invariably on E-flat. The result of the linear root among basic pitches of the melody, however, is on B-flat. According to Hindemith's theory of tonal gravity,[29] for purely acoustical reasons, B-flat can be considered the tonal center. Even if resorting to the conventional interpretation of the tonal center of *ujo,* which is E-flat, *whang-chong,* the vocal cadence is not on the tonal center.

On the other hand, the *kaemyonjo* is based on three basic notes which appear frequently and as structural notes of the music: B-flat, E-flat and A-flat. Other notes such as C, F and D-flat appear in recordings and even in notation. But these notes are only part of the abundant gracenotes and "bent" notes. They are neither stable nor frequent enough to be included in a regular pitch spectrum. It should be recognized that the *kaemyonjo* mode consists of three notes, B-flat, E-flat and A-flat, with a nebula of secondary pitches. Vocal melodic cadences of movements are always on A-flat while the postludes always rest on E-flat. Again, the result of an analysis of linear root among the basic pitches of a movement in *kaemyonjo* shows that the gravity focus is placed on A-flat. The tonality focus of A-flat is confirmed by the melodic cadences of vocal line but not with the postludes.

The conclusiveness of cadence that was stereotypical in the music of the West does not exist in *kagok*. This is due to the uniqueness of tonal organization of *ujo* and *kaemyonjo*, and a unique cadential practice that lacks uniform confirmation of a cadential pitch. The complaint of inexperienced listeners about this inconclusiveness may be justified.

The excellence of the modes was claimed for centuries, as in *Paekunam Kumbo,*[30] *Ch'onggu Yongon,*[31] *Kukak Taejonjip,*[32] *Haedong Kayo,*[33] and *Kagok Wonryu.*[34] All claimed the music in *ujo* to be magnificent, transparent, peaceful, harmonious, profound and pleasant. On the other hand, music in *kaemyonjo* was judged to be wretched, mournful, desolate, sad, and sentimental.

The other musical genre using *sijo* poems is the *Sijo-ch'ang,* which is shorter and performed by a singer or a singer and a drum, *changgo.* The *sijo-ch'ang* belongs to the grass roots of the society. In this *sijo-ch'ang,* only *kaemyonjo* is used. The melodic contour is basically stepwise in its scale formation. Undulating motion of melismatic melodies is comparatively simple except for abundant gracenotes, the effect of which will be discussed later. In most movements except *p'yon-rak, p'yon-su-dae-yop, on-rak, u-p'yon, whan-kae-rak,* long sustained notes in the melodic line are not unusual. Notes of five to seven beats are frequently found, while one note in each movement (the end of the fourth chapter in most compositions) is held for fourteen beats.

The static effect of the melodic line is magnified by the unique style of textual setting. For the 121 beats of vocal activity in a movement, up to forty-eight syllables of *p'yong-sijo* of poem are set. Moreover, the first two syllables of each poetic foot are presented in the manner of "head thrust," which is to open a phrase with an accent, often with a gracenote and close together. An example is:

Tong-ch'ang- - - - - - - - - - - -i

Such practice causes clarity of the text at the beginning of each poetic foot but increases the melismatic effect as a whole.

An unique singing style is also applied for static effect. After the initial thrust of each poetic foot, the singer's introduction of the following syllables is very gradual in diction. Most of the diphthongs, and any phonemes that can be broken down to be treated as diphthongs, are separated into the smallest nuclear phonemes and introduced at different points in the melody. This stylized singing method is characteristic in *kagok*. Thus the melismatic effect is created by phonetic slides.

Chromaticism in *kagok* repertoire is negligible. However, the technique of modulation is used in such movements as *pan-yop, p'yon-rak* and *whan-kae-rak*. These are the pieces located between the movements in *ujo* mode and movements in *kae-myonjo* mode in the suite.

In addition to the texture, tempo, and rhythm, the above melodic style, contour, long sustained notes, stylized singing method and diatonicism, all seem to contribute toward a static, courtly and introspective musical effect.

The movements with *chang-sijo,* developed during the later period, are not always fast. But the movements in ten-beat rhythmic pattern are always in the fast tempo. *P'yon-rak, p'yon-su-dae-yop, on-p'yon,* and *u-p'yon* movements are with the ten-beat rhythmic patterns in fast *tempo. Whan-kae-rak* movement has fast, sixteen-beat rhythm patterns. These five movements do not have such long sustained notes as the slow movements and are more rhythmic. However, due to the similarity in the type of texture, the general melodic contour, stylized singing and diatonicism, these movements are still in the vein of classical *kagok* style, with some modernization.

It is remarkable how artistic interest sustains such a slow and static music. If the music can be explained aesthetically on the relative basis of tension relaxation, the feeling of relaxation is the prevailing mood of *kagok*. Then what are the elements creating tension?

The general character of Korean language and poetry is the placement of a thrusting accent on the first syllable of a word. The last syllable of a sentence is the weakest syllable of all in terms of accent. The statistical analysis of a hundred-and-one folk songs of *Minyo Samch'olri*,[35] shows that ninety-nine songs start on the down beat while two songs cannot be decided as they are non-metric. Sixty-nine songs have their last syllables on a weak metric position, thirty songs on a rather stronger metric position, and two songs are non-metric. In a further analysis of the thirty songs it is found that the last words of the texts consist of one or two syllables of the verb followed by two syllables of suffix. In these cases, the first syllable of the verb is placed on a strong metric position and, due to the nature of the arrangement of syllables, the last syllable of the suffix happens to appear on a strong metric position. As a whole, it may be observed that a characteristic of Korean music is to start on the strong beat and end on a weaker metric position.

The use of these characteristics of Korean poetry, combined with the initial thrust of each phrase (as previously mentioned), is an important method of creating subtle tension in *kagok*. This is extended by singing simple sustained notes, usually introduced with *sforzando* then decreasing in intensity. This is a diametrically opposing singing practice to that of western music, which sustains a note with full voice to the end or even has a *crescendo-decrescendo* feature.

The abundant grace notes are used effectively in creating subtle ripples in the slow-moving melodic lines. Tastefully and well-placed grace notes (one to four), are a point of aesthetical appreciation and add textural beauty to the music. Another aesthetical embellishment of melody is the trill, almost always employed toward the end of each long sustained melodic line and starting without any *vibrato*.

As a result, tension and artistic interest is created by the head thrust of each phrase, the exaggerated changes of dynamics in the form of *sforzando,* grace notes, the method of sustaining and ending long notes, and vocal coloring. However, these are so subtle that they create a quasi-textural aesthetic dimension rather than an expressionistic goal.

While it is said that any *sijo* can be sung to any movement of *kagok,* in practice, there are certain combinations. It was believed that each movement of *kagok* has its own unique ethos. The description in *Ch'onggu Yongon* of Kim Ch'ontaek, *Haedong Kayo* of Kim Sujang, and *Kagok Wonryu* of Pak Hyogwan and An Minyong are almost identical. In the three anthologies, the ethos of seventeen movements are given. Some of the descriptions are:

MUSIC	DESCRIPTION
Ch'o-jung-dae-yop	Like southern breeze on stringed instrument. Like floating cloud and running water.
I-jung-dae-yop	Like a lonely sail in the ocean. Like a broad river embracing a rapid.
Sam-jung-dae-yop	Like a hero on a swift horse. Like throwing a stone from a high mountain.

Even if *sijo* has a great amount of physical description, the communicative focus of the poem may often be found beyond the limitations of semantics. Often, *sijo* is considered to be symbolic.

In the choice of a poem to be set to music, it seems obvious that the mode in which the music is composed became the guideline. It is assumed that a selection procedure took place by a well-versed singer, in a similar way to that of a composer selecting a poem for his work.[36] The symbolic, or even metaphysical focus of *sijo* made it easy to combine with the music that which is neither descriptive nor limiting in expression. Therefore, the total coherence of poem and music may hardly exist in general terms, let alone the effect of tone-painting. However, it might not have been necessary after all, due to the nature of poems (especially *p'yong-sijo*) and music. In fact, the broadness of musical expression and the symbolic quality of poetry complement each other to create yet a higher aesthetic goal. In the case of *kagok,* the aesthetic theory of H. Kretzschmar explains the role of music.[37]

> Music not as substitute for the pictorical arts or for objects of nature, but rather for poetry, i.e., as a *Sprachkunst* of lesser clarity, but of finer shades and deeper effects, than the ordinary language.

This is a combination of the theories of the autonomy and the heteronomy of musical art.

Conclusion

The virtue of music is its ability to create a unique beauty that no other artistic medium can create. Man has attempted to describe this Ultimate Beauty, with realistic description, poetry, visual assistance, and metaphysical symbolism. But success was limited to the description of the peripheral outline and general concept of the Ultimate Beauty. This is the territory of intuition and experience. In *kagok,* poems and sounds should be called the physical form that is used to express the content. Then, in turn, the content is to imply the Ultimate Beauty.

The physical characteristics of the form are calmness, slow *tempi,* melodic and textural melisma, a plain dynamic level as a whole, lack of climactical outburst, and heterophony. Sensual balance is created by subtlety; frequent short dynamic thrusts with the use of the initial syllable of a phrase or of grace notes: trills; voice coloring, and a constantly changing texture created by heterophony. "Pine leaves rustling in the forest" is another description by many musicians. On the other hand, the *p'yong-sijo,* a uniquely rhythmed verse, deals with subject such as loyalty, panegyric matters, nature, didactic matters, *feng-liu,* and love.

Such a physical arrangement of sounds and music can best be summarized as expressing simplicity, solemnness, naturalness and grace. Other qualities that may be more difficult to define are optimism, detachment, straightforwardness, intellectualism and introspectiveness. Another often used sentence to describe the form is "motion in stillness," i.e., "energy in calmness." In the *kagok* movements, in slow and medium *tempi,* it is clear that emotionality is lacking.

On the other hand *p'yong-sijo* can be summarized as having various expressions: simplicity, solemnness, naturalness, grace, optimism, impersonality, straightforwardness, intellectuality, introspectiveness, and lyricism. These expressions parallel that of the music. Other expressions that are more difficult to define in music but are clear in poetry are the concept of morality, righteousness, and vacuous quiescence. The Neo-Confucian philosophy of emancipation from the *Ch'ing* (selfish desire), which can be cited easily in *sijo,* may be linked easily in music where emotionality is lacking in *kagok.*

If music is less clear but deeper in expression, with finer shades, certainly the combination of *p'yong-sijo* and *kagok* music reached another plateau of aesthetics that could not have been achieved solely by poetry or music. Then, as previously stated, the Ulitmate Beauty of *kagok* on *p'yong-sijo* exists beyond this expression—the Content.

With the advent of *chang-sijo,* emotionalism, pessimism and hedonistic views were reflected in the poetry. A mild tendency of *stilus theatralis* is felt for the first time in *kagok.* The music responded to this new expression by inventing faster music and music in more rhythmic ten-beat basic rhythmic pattern to accomodate the new poetry. However, other aspects of music demonstrate that the music, in general, remained more conservative.

It should be noted that, like that of other artistic media, the aesthetics of music of any time period is always strongly influenced by the philosophy of the time.

Notes

1. Other vocal music in this category are *kasa* and *sijo-ch'ang.*
2. Other vocal music in this category are *p'ansori, chapga.*
3. Translation by Fung Yu-Lan, *A Short History of Chinese Philosophy* (New York: The Free Press, 1948).
4. Kim Busik, *Samguk Sagi* (1145) (The History of the Three Kingdoms: Silla, Paekjae and Koguryo).
5. 樂也者 聖人之 所樂也
6. Ch'eng Yi (程頤) (1033-1108) and Ch'eng Hao (程顥) (1032-1085).
7. Fung Yu-Lan, *A Short History of Chinese Philosophy* (New York: The Free Press, 1948), p. 297.
   For every kind of thing there is the *Li,* which makes it what it is ought to be. The *Li* is the *chi* of that thing, i.e., it is its ultimate standard. (The word *chi* originally was a name for the ridge pole at the peak of the roof of a building. As used in Neo-Confucianism, it means the highest ideal prototype of things.) For the

universe as a whole, there must also be an ultimate standard which is supreme and all embracing. It embraces the multitude of *Li* for all things and is the highest summation of all of them. Therefore, it is called the Supreme Ultimate of *T'ai-Chi.*

8. Music in *Saejong Sillok,* Vol. 136.

9. *Saejong Sillok,* Vol. 47.

10. *Songjong Sillok,* Vol. 219.

11. Pak Bong-sok, *Kuksa Chonghae* (Seoul: Pakyongsa, 1960).

12. Yi Whang, *Tosan Sibigok* (1565).
    In the preface: "There is too much obscene music in this country. Even though *Hanlim Byolgok* was written by an intellectual, still, this is lax without control, and of flirting character. It is not suitable for a learned man . . ."

13. In *Koryosa* (高麗史), Vol. 125 (1454 A.D.), it is stated that "Kim Wonsang made a *Sinjo* (新調)"; In *Akhak Kwaebom* (樂學軌範), (1475 A.D.), the word "*Ak-sijo*" is used.; In *Saejong Sillok* (世宗實錄), the word "*Ak-sijo*" (樂時調) is also used.

14. Yang Yom-kyu, *Kukmunhak Kaesol* (Seoul: Chongyon Sa, 1959).

15. "Ilwolun sosanae-jigo, Whanghanun Tonghaero dunda, . . ."

16. Yi Yi (李珥) and Yi Whang (李滉) were the most outstanding scholars.

17. An Sang, *Kum Hap-ja-bo* (琴合字譜) (Also commonly called *An Sang Kumbo* 安瑺琴譜), 1572.

18. So Myong-ing, comp., *Taeak Hubo,* 1758.

19. Yi Tukyun, comp., *Hyongum Tongmun Yugi* (玄琴東文類記), 1620.

20. Ibid.

21. Unknown, *Paekunam Kumbo,* preserved in Lee Hye Ku Library. See Lee Hye Ku, *Hankuk Umak Sosol* (Seoul: Seoul National University Press, 1967).

22. Lee, *op. cit.*

23. However, *chung-dae-yop* still appears in *Kagok Wonryu* (歌曲源流), of 1876 by Pak Hyogwan and An Minyong. Disappearance is noted in *Hyongum Oum T'ongron* (玄琴五音統論) of 1886 by Yun Yonggu.

24. Kim Sujang, *Haedong Kayo* (海東歌謠), 1763: So Yugo, *Yuyaeji* (遊藝志), between 1725-1767; Song Kyae, *Kogum Kagok* (古今歌曲), 1764.

25. Lee Hye Ku, Song Kyongrin and Yi Changbae, *Kukak Taejonjib* (國樂大全集) (Seoul: Sinseki Record Co., 1968).

26. It is quite usual that the name of the poet of *chang-sijo* is not known.

27. Lee Chuwhan, *Kagokbo* (歌曲譜) (Seoul: Kukrib Kukakwon, 1959).

28. Movements in ten-beat pattern are *P'yon-rak, P'yon-su-dae-yop, U-p'yon* and *On-p'yon.*

29. Paul Hindemith, *Craft of Musical Composition* (New York: Associated Music, 1945).

30. Unknown, *Paekunam Kumbo* (白雲庵琴譜), preserved in Lee Hye Ku library. See Lee Hye Ku, *Hanguk Umak Sosol.*

31. Kim Ch'on T'aek, *Ch'onggu Yongon* (青丘永言), (1727).

32. Lee Hye Ku, Song Kyongrin and Lee Ch'angbae, *Kukak Taejonjip.*

33. Kim Changsu, *Haedong Kayo* (海東歌謠), (1736).

34. Pak Hyogwan and An Minyong, *Kagok Wonryu* (歌曲源流), (1876).

35. Song Kyungrin, Lee Ch'angbae and Kim Kisu, *Minyo Samch'olri* (民謠三千里) (Seoul: Sungumsa, 1968).

36. Julius Bahle, *Der Musikalische Schaffensprozess* (Leipzig: 1936).

    In the experiment on motivation of creativity, Bahle provided three poems of different poets and subjects for each of a number of composers. Then he observes the factors that make composers determine the selection of a poem. Composers selected a particular poem because the poem was sympathetic to his "experience," "value" and "encouraging."

37. W. Apel, *Harvard Dictionary of Music* (Cambridge: Harvard University Press, 1944), p. 17.

7 / The Lady Fortunetellers of Korea's Cities: There is a Mysterious Woman in Your Future

BARBARA YOUNG

Fortunetellers with Spirit

Not exactly shamans, not quite priests, not really astrologers, and not licensed psychotherapists, the women who earn their living telling fortunes in Korea's cities offer advice, insights, and interpretations to a kaleidoscope of clientele. They are marginal in many senses—for instance, they are not fully approved by government officials, by the educated "elite," and by certain religious leaders, and they are not easily categorized as one or another standard type of religious practitioner. Yet these fortunetellers do a healthy though seasonal business despite their problematical status. Known in Korea as *yo chomchaengi* or, more politely as *chomsulga,* they add a vivid, vital dimension to Seoul's already richly diverse urban life. Their role and functions surpass local color, however. Fortunetellers the world over (and Korea is no exception) have their detractors, but I do not count myself one of them. As perpetuators of a stubbornly persistent tradition offering a continuously popular service, Korea's lady fortunetellers wear many hats (and for those of you who know Korean shamans, I should say that I speak in the figurative sense): they counsel, cajol, scold, sympathize, entertain, comfort, listen, argue, and take money for it. Indeed, much is made of this latter fact, especially by government officials who present themselves as pro-modernization, not anti-religious (i.e., "no wasteful and extravegant rituals"). Not wanting to appear anti-religious myself, nor pro-modernization-at-any-cost, nor for that matter reactionary (i.e., "keep Korea's fortunetellers traditional"), I present the following observations as an unabashedly positive view of traditional divination. In this short paper, I will focus on features, functions, style and status of one type of diviner in Seoul—the *chomchaengi.*[1]

Without delving into etymologies which I'll leave to linguists and native speakers, I should say at the outset that in my experience in Seoul, there are two uses of the word *"chomchaengi."*[2] (For those who don't know Korean, *-chaengi* is a derogatory suffix meaning "person skilled at" and *chom* refers to divination, especially divination by reading portents.) On the one hand, the term *"chomchaengi"* has a generic referent which is roughly "anyone who does any kind of fortunetelling." In this usage, shamans, horoscope readers, palm, face and name readers, *Book of Change* interpreters, bird diviners, and coin or rice readers are all subsumed under the category of *"chomchaengi."* On the other hand, some (particularly diviners themselves) use the term with a more specific referent in mind, namely, "those who divine by interpreting omens, portents, or signs of the spirit world." This, of course, opens a whole can of slippery questions devolving on which signs are produced by spirits, but generally speaking, birthdates, bodily features, and names are exempt. This leaves, mainly, coin readers and rice readers. In fact the overlapping referents of this one term not only confuse anthropologists, but also give rise to some curious but understandable inconsistencies, such as Christian clients who patronize only horoscope diviners because their pastors have admonished them to forsake *chom* (which they interpret as divination by portents). At any rate, the *chomchaengi* who are the subject of this paper are the latter group: those who specialize in performing divinations which interpret the messages and actions of spirits. (And if there are any *chomchaengi* reading, please forgive me for using the less polite form of reference; *chomsulka* is so formal, I found, that most Seoul citizens don't respond to it as they do to *"chomchaengi."*)

Style and Features: A Woman for All Seasons

How does one know a *chomchaengi* when one sees one? What exactly do they do to divine the future? In fact, one can only recognize these fortunetellers in their professional settings; on the street they look like anyone else. However, their personal lives are characterized by spiritual experiences which they learn to harness for purposes of divination. A description of a few individuals out of the forest of *chomchaengi* may do more than a summary of characteristics.

Case 1. A Rice Reader

Mrs. Song, now thirty years old, has been a professional diviner for eight years. Born into a Christian family in Seoul, she tells fortunes, she explains, "because of an illness I suffered when I was twelve." When she recovered from this sickness, driven on by a vision she experienced, she left home and went into the mountains in Kangwon Province. There she practiced asceticism and spiritual discipline (*sudo* 修道), while her parents back in Seoul registered her at the Police Department as a lost child. After a year she returned home, again took up residence with her parents, and attended junior and senior high school. She attended college, married, bore two children, and all the while made uncannily accurate predictions about the future of her acquaintances and political leaders. Attaining some notoriety from this talent, she was sought out by friends and strangers, the couple moving three times to escape what her husband saw as an unseemly business. Still clients were dogged, and finally her husband allowed her to divine professionally. She claims she has mastered no special technique, does not study, and has read no books on the subject. She had never been initiated as a shaman, nor does she consider herself one. By *yongkam* (靈感 spiritual inspiration) alone, she says, she can foretell the future. She prays three times a day to a "god who is like a Buddhist spirit, but is not part of the Buddhist pantheon." Each morning she prays before a green curtained altar bright with paper flowers, brass and aluminum bowls, bells, and candlesticks behind which is a painting of the spirit who assists her—an ephemeral-looking figure in swirling robes, oval face encircled with light. In an armchair before this same altar, Mrs. Song receives clients. A divination begins with the following questions: What is your age? (Sometimes, do you know your *ddi?* animal sign.) When is your lunar birthday? Consulting no books or charts, Mrs. Song fingers a few grains of rice and seeds in a bowl before her. Without chanting or otherwise visibly calling the spirits, she continues to touch the rice and tells the client her fortune without much conversation:

> Your bad fortune is almost past. Your situation will be bad until the sixth lunar month of this year. In the seventh or eight month you will move to a different house or change your surroundings. In the ninth and tenth

months your outlook on society will be good but your health will be bad and you will have the bad luck to be verbally abused (people will gossip about you). During the eleventh and twelfth months you should absolutely not travel. You can change your citizenship. The best job for you would be some kind of service work. Next year everything will be good. You have the fortune to travel. Don't hesitate to do this, for only if you do will the road to advancement be clear and your future good. If you have something special you want to know, ask me.

Client: I am still not married. When will I go to my husband's family? (When will I marry?)

Diviner: Next year either you will marry or you will travel. Next year you will decide. The *ddi* (animal sign) that would match well with yours (Dragon) are Tiger, Chicken, Monkey, and Dragon.

Client: These days I am attending graduate school. Will I achieve success by studying?

Diviner: Yes. According to your *p'alcha* (eight characters), your destiny is to lead people. You can also serve people. Many difficult crises remain for you but in the end you will succeed.

Client: I've been lazy lately. I haven't been working on my thesis.

Diviner: From last year to this year, your direction has been aimless, wandering. From next summer, from the sixth month to the seventh or eighth, you will settle down.

Client: I would like to study in America.

Diviner: Do it¡ You have the fortune to do it. Whether you travel alone or participate in a formal program, you are able to go.

Client: Next year in May there is a chance, a special program, but there are so many competitors, I don't know . . .

Diviner: It's a possibility. You'll be able to go somehow.

Mrs. Song asks the client if there are further questions, explains that the amount of the fee is optional (pointing to a huge stack of paper money), and asks the client to send up from the downstairs waiting room the person next in line.

Case 2. A Coin Reader

Mrs. Pak, a grandmother whose round unwrinkled face belies

her age, moved to Seoul from Kangnung many years ago, but is a
new resident of a tiny house with two rooms and a cooking area in
the countyard. She cares for and financially supports several of her
youngest children, for she is separated from her husband. She has
been telling fortunes for three years, ever since a spirit came down
to her, which she describes as follows: "I went mad by accident. On
the sixth of May I went mad and on the twenty-first of that month,
I told fortunes. My spirit is *Chungguk tongja kuisin* (Chinese child
spirit).'' One of the rooms in her house contains an altar, behind
which are printed posters of *sansin* (the mountain spirit), *ch'ilsong*
(seven stars spirit), *yongwang* (dragon king), *taesin* (spirit of an
ancestor shaman), and *obang sinchang* (five direction general-
spirit). There she prays and divines for clients using, alternatively,
rice, coins, and a bowl of water. She usually confines her divinations to the morning. With a client sitting on a cushion before her,
she lights incense and eight candles on the altar. She places two
rosaries around her neck and one short one on her wrist. She brings
out a small table on which sits a small bowl of rice and seven coins.
She rocks back and forth, shakes the coins in her hands, begins
chanting, and throws down the coins. Still chanting, she scoops
them up and tosses them again, repeating this for several minutes.
Suddenly she whistles, her voice changing pitch as she speaks. (An
old lady helps the client understand her babytalk.)

Diviner: This year from the fifth to the seventh lunar month, do
you intend to travel?

Client: Yes, in July or August.

Diviner: You will have sunshine this year. You will be well known.
You will have many followers. There are two of you staying in Seoul?

Client: Yes, my sister and I.

Diviner: You cannot go back home together. Marrying one person
is not good. This year in the ninth lunar month, you will
meet a good husband. If you don't marry this year, you
will marry in two or three years. You must go to another
place.

Client: Where?

Diviner: To hometown (old lady interprets). No! No! To church!

Client: No, I don't go to church.

Diviner: This year you should pray to a wood or stone Buddha.

Because you have a good fortune this year, everywhere you go and everything you do is good. You are good hearted and you receive people's respect, but you do not have an easy time with personal relationships. You have only one parent? Is that right? Do you have two?

Client: I have two.

Diviner: You have parents but you must forget one. If you marry, you must live away from your parents. This year your fortune is to take some examination and if you take it, you will pass. It will be in the tenth lunar month, or the second lunar month of next year. You will attain a high position when you are 37 or 38. Will you go to Japan? You should travel all around the world. You have no fortune for business. In order to succeed you must study. You must work hard to succeed. Last year you met a good man. Why didn't you marry him?

Client: I don't know who you mean.

Diviner: Ask me questions!

Client: Will I have sons?

Diviner: You will have only one child. (Her voice normal again.) If you want to have a child, you should worship a wood or stone Buddha this year. Keep it on your table. Pick a number (holding open a book for the client). Your fortune is five. (Reading) Beware of some injury or loss. If you move to the east, you will never have to worry about food or clothes. No one understands your difficult situation because it does not concern them. Who will break off the mud that is stuck on your clothes? (Puts down book.) Your fortune this year is confining. You want to achieve everything faster but you can't. It would be best if you marry this year. The fortune to marry has already come. Last year you had the fortune to go to a match-maker; didn't you go?

Client: No, I didn't.

Mrs. Pak signals the end of her inspiration by her voice change and by putting aside the small table, coins, and rosaries. Asked about her profession, she explains that she learned how to tell fortunes on her own, with no instruction from a teacher. She has no *sinomoni* (spirit mother), she says, and has never been initiated as a shaman. She cannot perform shaman ceremonies such as *kut* although she celebrates Buddha's birthday, the seventh day of the seventh lunar month, and the ninth day of the ninth lunar month: "I only have celebrations on these special days, and they are not really *kut*. I don't like *kut*. I hate to see *kut*. We all have the same job but it's not suitable for me. I only have the *tongja* (child spirit) clothes. This place is just like a village shrine (*songnangdang*). It's the same here as a temple."[3] Offering prayers for clients and performing divinations for clients are Mrs. Pak's only source of income.

Case 3. Another Rice Reader

Mrs. Kim, a gray-haired diminuitive woman of fifty-four, commutes by bus everyday to a closet-sized office in downtown Seoul. Though in this office there is barely room for a *yontán* (charcoal) stove, a small altar, her divination table, herself, and one client, she has told fortunes in this location for four years. It has been fifteen years in all since she took up the profession of prophecy, though it was many years earlier that she was first afflicted with a spirit—"intoxicated by a *kuisin,*" (spirit or ghost) as she puts it. The apparition first came to her when she was twenty-two and caused her months of fainting spells, weakness, and "uncontrollable murmuring." Married, with several children, she left her husband when she was thirty-five and moved to Seoul (shortly after that she was widowed). She joined the Christian Church, becoming a deaconess, and had a series of operations which failed to cure her illness. She was told by a shaman that according to her *saju* ("four pillars" or in less literal translation, horoscope), she must become either a *kisaeng* (entertainer) or a *mudang* (shaman): she could not resist her fate. She first began telling fortunes in order to earn money for cigarettes, travel, and so on. She found that all her physical problems disappeared when she became a *chomchaengi* (though she used the term "*chomsulga*"). Having completed only two years of primary school, she does not read and has never had a teacher of divination techniques: "I learned by force of the *kuisin,*" she says. A divination by Mrs. Kim is done using a small pile of rice she keeps tied in a red cloth. Unwrapping the rice, she puts it in a corner of a small table and puts the table on the red cloth. The client's fee is set out near the table and the diviner tosses out a few grains of rice as she asks the client's age. Occasionally flicking out additional rice and poking at the arrangement of grains, she rapidly outlines her predictions:

Diviner: You are twenty-five then?

Client: Yes.

Diviner: You should marry someone older, someone now 32 or 37. In the early days of your life, you will be lonesome even though you live with your parents. After you meet your husband, you will be happy. You will meet your husband either this year or when you are 27. Your life expectancy is 80. Your husband will have an occupation demanding a particular skill. Your *saju* is very strong. You will have four sons, two of whom will have great success. In the coming year a happy accident will occur in the eleventh or twelfth lunar month. Perhaps you will marry then.

Mrs. Kim, who charges a very low fee for her divinations, says she is satisfied with the number of clients she has, though she averages only two per day. When she has no customers, she sleeps on her *ondol* (heated) floor, prays to the seven star spirit and to heaven, and visits occupants of the small shops in the vicinity of her office. She knows a few other *chomchaengi* and although she sometimes thinks of herself as a shaman, she has had no initiation or formal apprenticeship. She is not a member of any divination association. She is not as popular a fortuneteller as a male diviner nearby, she says, because she does not do "philosophical explanations."

Case 4. Another Coin Reader

Mrs. Nam, like Mrs. Kim, rents a small room downtown which includes a curtained alcove with a fairly sizeable altar. The altar itself, upon which are plaster statues of Buddha in addition to posters of the mountain spirit and the shaman spirit, betrays a stronger Buddhist emphasis than do many *chomchaengi's* offices. The signs on Mrs. Nam's door—*"Sin Chom"* (spirit divination) and *"Sinkido"* (prayer, devotions)—also suggest that Mrs. Nam is a *chomchaengi* with a Buddhist orientation, a *posal,* as she likes to be called. Unlike Mrs. Kim, however, who commutes to her downtown office, Mrs. Nam lives in this one partitioned room with her high school aged son and daughter. A hatch under the paper covered wooden floor holds a *yontan* (charcoal) stove which can be pulled out for cooking and for heat in the winter. (This household and four other diviners in similar rooms around a central courtyard share the water spigot and toilet). Now fifty-four years old, Mrs. Nam was born in the northern part of Korea, married at an early age, and fled to Pusan' when the Korean War broke out. She had been telling fortunes for a living for fifteen years, using a technique she describes as "murmurs and whispers using beads and coins." She explains how she came to take up this profession as follows:

> When I was seventeen, I was very sick and also I married that same year. Whenever I bore a child, it died. I wanted to know why so I went to a *chomchaengi*. Everyone said this happened because heavenly spirits descended to me. I was sick until I was thirty-nine years old, when I became a *posal*. When I began this job, it took only a half an hour for me to recover. Since that time I have been all right.

She had four teachers (not spirit mothers, she said, but other fortunetellers) who lived in a district in downtown Seoul which has since been demolished. Averaging four to six customers a day (though summer is very slow), she is a member of the Association of Diviners whose membership is primarily composed of male *sajuchaengi* (horoscope diviners): she explained this association by saying that she does *saju* and *kunghap* (horoscopes and compatability analysis) and face reading while she divines with the help of a spirit. Four times a year she visits a temple on a mountaintop outside of Seoul. She observes Buddhist holidays and certain calendrical holidays (such as the beginning of spring) by making a small offering of food at her altar (and sometimes playing cymbals). She suggests that her divination technique includes two important elements: 1) "something descends from heaven" (she adds that this cannot be taught or learned), and 2) her own philosophy, acquired by reading books on divination. A fortune told by Mrs. Nam begins with her lighting a stick of incense. She asks the client's birthdate as she puts a long strand of wooden beads around her neck. She looks briefly at a *"hwangap chek"* (sixty year cycle book) in order to learn the dominant factor in the client's horoscope.[4] As she does so, the client outlines her situation:

Client: I am now fifty-four years old and many people have said to me that my *sajup'alcha* is very strong. Sometimes I have heard 'You will marry two or three times.' But I have always solved my problems with my own effort. According to my own philosophy, the marriage which my parents chose for me should end by the death of both parties, so therefore there is only one man for me. I was once engaged in business; I worked in a bus company, a restaurant, raising pigs, and in a taffy factory. Through the last of these jobs, I earned 300 million *won,* but I resigned and gave management rights to my husband. In three years there was nothing left. Because of business failure and a lawsuit which caused a great illness, my husband died. During the time we were married, several accidents happened (for instance, our house caught on fire, one child was hit by a car, etc.). Later I found out my husband had a mistress. All this time I perservered. I want to know the future. I do not expect filial piety *(hyoyang)* from my son. Last year I spent all the money left by my husband and now I feel sadness. My son? He is Sign of the Rat.

The diviner picks up a short rosary and rotates it in one hand, mumbling under her breath: "This person's son is Chang Un Sook, he lives in Masan in the south near Pusan, his age is twenty-nine, he is Sign of the Rat, he wants to know his fortune for the Year of the Snake." She picks up thirteen large coins and slaps them down on a small table. Chanting all the while, she scoops them up and throws them down, suddenly opening her eyes and saying:

Diviner: Next month he will have good karma or fate *(inyon).*

Client: This is his situation: He finished the college course in law and graduated from Yonsei University. Four firms (three in Seoul and one in Masan) offered him a job. He chose the one in Masan because of the good working conditions there. In the long run, which one would be more advantageous for him—here or Masan?

Diviner: The twentieth day of the first month is all right for moving. If he moves around this time, he can get a promotion. After the promotion, he will be prosperous.

Client: What about my eldest daughter? She is Sign of the Rabbit, born the 27th day of the 7th month.

Diviner: (Throwing the coins down a few time, without chanting.) Roughly speaking, this girl's fortune is: Material but no good leads to change. She must move here and there.

Client: She is already married.

Diviner: What is her husband's age?

Client: Thirty.

Diviner: In that case, your daughter's fortune is to have more family members and more material fortune. This year is *samjae* (period of misfortune) for her. If she receives her *samjae* fortune well, she can spend her time as usual. Her husband's luck is ascending.

Client: Now they live in the United States.
Diviner: You want them to come here next March or April but you
              cannot meet them then. Instead, you can have a reunion
              in July or August. Then they can live happily. Your-son-
              in-law has good opportunities then.

The divination continues with the woman asking about her second
daughter and her boyfriend and ends with a question about the
client visiting her son in Masan: "Which is better, going or not going?" Jangling the coins on the table, the diviner replies that the
woman's luck is "changing" so going would be good unless she
were to go to the southeast, a response which satisfies the client
who relinquishes her place in front of the diviner to another
woman. Mrs. Nam, whose divinations are modestly priced but not
cheap, supports herself and her two children by divinations alone,
performing no other services for fees (the religious rituals she does
are for herself and her family). She does not stress the economic
aspects of her work, however, but the spiritual and physical ones:
her profession is responsible for curing her illness and preventing a
relapse.

What these four women have in common, in addition to their sex,
is their experience of illness, interpreted as spiritual and eventually
controlled through spiritual means. *Chomchaengi,* as opposed to
horoscope diviners (and other diviners who do not predict using
spiritual insights), are generally women; they usually have had little
education, they occupy a very low status in society, and after suffering *mubyong* (shaman sickness), they earn their living divining
by inspiration. Coins or rice combined with chanting are frequently
the means by which they grasp the spirits' view of the client's life
and situation. In sociological and technical ways (such as in terms
of their status, their spiritual experiences, and their divining
methods), *chomchaengi* are very similar to shamans though func-
tionally their sphere of influence is much narrower, as is the social
context in which they work. Shamans offer a host of religious
rituals in addition to divination, while for *chomchaengi,* divination
is their main occupation (usually their sole income producing activity) and their main outlet for expressing their spiritual insights.[5]

FUNCTIONS: How're They Gonna Keep 'Em Down on the Farm?

If my research in Seoul in 1976 and 1977 is any indication, as it should be, given Korea's rapidly increasing urbanization, professional spirit diviners do not and will not live and work only in villages. A shaman or two may be able to earn a living in a small village, but it seems to take a market town to support two or three professional *chomchaengi*. And if *chomchaengi* survive in market towns, they positively thrive in cities. (In fact, it might be argued that urban areas produce the conditions necessary for *chomchaengi* to earn a living.) Though there are also shamans in large cities, *chomchaengi* may very well be seen as urban shamans. That is, a *chomchaengi* is essentially a shaman (perhaps initiated, perhaps not) who specializes in divination.[6] Consider the similarities:
——Both shamans and *chomchaengi* are usually women.
——Both often have had little formal education.
——Both occupy a low status in society.
——Both shamans and *chomchaengi* are often social anomalies in terms of their role in their immediate family. Weathering society's disapproval, these women frequently are husbandless (due to either death or separation) and act as heads of household, supporting themselves and their children with the income from their profession.
——Both shamans and *chomchaengi* assert that they do not choose their occupation, but have it thrust upon them. Afflicted by an illness later identified by others as *mubyong* (shaman sickness), most shamans and *chomchaengi* express what seems to be a kind of psychological imperative to perform their low status work.
——Most importantly, both shamans and *chomchaengi* divine using a mediumistic technique. The key element in divinations by both is interpreting the actions and will of spirits in a client's life. Yet consider the differences:
——*Chomchaengi* usually divine for individuals, while shamans (especially rural shamans) often divine for the whole family, or at least know the client's whole family. This is a double edged sword: shamans have access to greater information about a client's situation, but they are also more accountable to the client and client's family following rituals or divinations. This may lead to a dif-

ference in strategies of divination, and perhaps in part accounts for the *chomchaengi's* specialization in divination rather than treatment.

——*Chomchaengi* work in a climate of anonymity, while shamans are often part of a social network which includes clients. Shamans, unlike *chomchaengi,* often have a fluctuating but fairly permanent following, making completely private divinations more difficult than for *chomchaengi,* who often work in greater isolation.

——*Chomchaengi* work in offices during business hours, while shamans work where they live. *Chomchaengi* can thus maintain slightly more distance from their profession and can even keep their children, if they so desire, from seeing them at work. In terms of family life, being a *chomchaengi* may be slightly less disruptive than being a shaman.

——*Chomchaengi* offer a more limited range of services, usually only divination, while shamans do much more—divination plus large and small ceremonies for healing, for luck, to placate the ancestors, to mourn a death, to comfort individuals (both living and dead), and so on.

——*Chomchaengi* are paid monetary fees, while shamans (especially rural shamans) may operate on something approximating a barter system, exchanging divinations and rituals for food or other services, thereby maintaining an on-going relationship with clients. While on the face of it, due to the high cost of some shaman ceremonies, being a shaman might seem more lucrative than being a *chomchaengi,* in fact there seems to be evidence to the contrary. Several city shamans, for instance, told me they now do only divinations because the high overhead on ceremonies (paying for food, musicians, etc.) leaves nothing left for them. Expenses for ritual paraphenalia are also much greater for shamans than chomchaengi who often wear ordinary street clothes.

——*Chomchaengi* usually learn their trade from a teacher, but they serve no formal apprenticeship and do not necessarily experience an initiation ceremony, while shamans usually go through more formal stages of training to attain professional standing. Maintenance of spiritual or kinship-like ties between teacher and student also seems less frequent among *chomochaengi* then among shamans.

In short, the essential element of the two occupations—spiritual inspiration—is the same, while the two social roles
are slightly different. *Chomchaengi* differ from shamans in degree
of services and training and in kind of relationship to clients,
clients' families, and teachers. *Chomchaengi* offer only a small
portion of the services that shamans do and they can perform their
occupation without much in the way of formal recognition or
group acceptance. They can merely hang up a shingle, if they wish,
while shamans gain clients, prestige, confidence, moral support,
and necessary referrals through their association with already
established shamans. *Chomchaengi* thus often operate in a much
more autonomous fashion than do shamans, who generally employ
musicians, assistants, and other shamans during their ceremonies
and often attract a following of clients and other apprentices.
Essentially the *chomchaengi*-client relationship is contractual:
anonymous, business-like, of limited duration, and discrete
(perhaps more discreet too, although city shamans can often provide equal obscurity). The *chomchaengi's* services are paid for in
full at each session and mutual obligations end when the client
leaves the diviner's office. Contrast this with the shaman who
works in a more familial or *gemeinshaftlicht* context: the shaman
knows of and about clients; she participates in a social network
which includes her own family and the clients' families; duration of
a session may be "extended" by social encounters in day-to-day
life; rituals are often performed in the client's home; and services
may be recompensed by exchanges instead of monetary payment
for each divination. A shaman is a religious specialist whose powers
include divination; a *chomchaengi* specializes in divinations which
have a religious basis but which are practiced in an essentially more
secular context. I would say that this mysterious woman looks like
a shaman in city garb.

To what can we attribute this specialization among shamans, if
indeed *chomchaengi* are to be seen in this way? Part of the answer
might be seen in the *chomchaengi's* role as adviser, listener, and
analyst (in a non-Freudian sense), services which are as much in demand in cities as in villages. A choice of schools for a high-school-
aged son or daughter? An upcoming marriage of a headstrong
young adult who is in love with someone unknown to the family?
Money lost through unfortunate investment? Moving to a new

house? Listless and stifled by events beyond one's control? Seeking a job? Arguing constantly with one's spouse? Suffering at the hands of one's mother-in-law? In love with a married woman? One's husband is staying out late every night? A *chomchaengi* will listen to these concerns and will express her opinions about them, pulling no punches, in fact. Yet full-blown shamans in cities and villages can meet these same needs, so functions alone cannot explain the specialization. Perhaps it's a matter of city style, or more specifically, social context. It would seem that the urban setting, coupled with the personal life situations and idiosyncracies of particular diviners, supports such a specialty in spirit divination without attendant religious rituals.

Simplistically put, advice without intervention may be the demand of city clients and a supply of *chomchaengi* has arisen to fill the need. Cities are crowded; families are simultaneously dispersed and crammed into small quarters; competition for jobs and education is keen; members of the opposite sex are thrown together in factories, schools, and on buses; literacy is widespread, making news and hype about different moral traditions readily available; streets are widened for traffic, houses are demolished, and persons and residences are displaced; as ever, children are born and not born; marriages are arranged, opposed, sought and broken; one's time is at a premium; one's income is never enough: in short, there are often more options and more choices to be made by urban than rural residents. In the face of such choices, who can overrate the appeal of talking things over with another person, especially someone not personally involved? Though many urban residents go to shamans for religious needs—prayers, supplications, particular rituals and ceremonies, illness and family troubles—as well as for divinations, many also desire the essentially secular (though inspired), impersonal, non-interventionist services of counselling, decision-making support, psychological comfort, social interaction, insights, and even entertainment which are provided by *chomchaengi*. There are, moreover, other places to turn for religious rituals—to Buddhist temples, Christian churches, to ceremonies honoring ancestors (for men), to personal prayer—but there are not many alternatives for divination. Friends, of course, can advise and listen; school alumni can counsel; employers can admonish; and almanacs can distinguish good days from bad, but who but a fortuneteller can warn and reassure about the future with any credibility?

At the same time that city conditions help create clients, the stress of urban situations may also bear down upon individual women provoking an illness that will be identified by neighbors, family members, and perhaps by a local shaman or *chomchaengi* as shaman sickness.[7] Preceded or followed by the economic necessity of supporting self and children, this illness may be channeled into an occupation; a woman may find it feasible to utilize this un-sought spirit in divination and other rituals. If there is a demand for divination, she may skip or shortcut full apprenticeship to a shaman and may succeed at earning a living doing divinations alone. In cities there seems to be enough demand for these services to support such divination specialists—*chomchaengi*—in addition to shamans. Moreover, official objections to traditional religious practices often hinge, nominally at least, on cost and noise, from both of which *chomchaengi* tend to be exempt. (Some *chomchaengi* have patrons who regularly give them gifts or large sums of money but these contributions are less obvious than those in payment for a ceremony which includes abundant food and clanging cymbals.)

In brief, becoming a shaman may offer a woman the follow-ing: 1) the attention and respect of a small segment of society, 2) a measure of independence from her immediate family and a means of earning a living, 3) fellowship of peers (somewhat less so for *chomchaengi*), 4) an explanation for hardships and a (perhaps tem-porary) diminution of responsibility, and 5) as suggested by I.M. Lewis, an opportunity to openly express frustrations, particularly with regard to status inequities.[8] However, for a woman living in the city, becoming a *chomchaengi* offers the following additional advantages: 1) lower visibility (and hence less criticism as a superstitious and evil influence), 2) potentially greater profit margin (depending upon one's skill), 3) easier attainment of profes-sional standing, and 4) a slightly greater chance of keeping one's occupation and family life separate (perhaps more true in the ideal than the actual world). The very fact that there are financially suc-cessful *chomchaengi* in Seoul in addition to successful shamans suggests the continuing need for the secular application of spiritual powers, which is a testimony to the strength of the spiritual tradi-tion itself. Moreover, it is an indication that traditional Korean in-stitutions can adapt and thrive in modern, urban, industrialized settings.

Status: The Double Bind

Through it all, however, both shamans and *chomchaengi* are victims of a kind of social double bind. Throughout Korea's history, those who act as intermediaries with spirits have been of the lowest social class. Though strict and visible social classes have faded somewhat, shamans and *chomchaengi* remain tainted (and, I might add, tend to draw members to their ranks from the economically depressed). Their continued low status is quite obvious if one talks to customers, non-customers, and diviners themselves. *Sajuchaengi* (persons who are skilled at interpreting horoscopes), for instance, quite vehemently insist that they are not *chomchaengi:* "What we do is not *chom"* (divination through portents), they say, "it is *cholhak"* (philosophy). Calling themselves *cholhakga* (philosophers), they do not wish to be considered the same as shamans or *chomchaengi.* They speak proudly of their knowledge of *Chuyok* (the *Book of Change*), but at the same time, many hide their true occupation from their children. Why? As a *sajuchaengi* explained, "My children will be ashamed of me, and they will be shunned by their friends at school."

Shamans and *chomchaengi* also express regrets at their low status. Many do not want their children to follow in their footsteps. Almost all say, "I did not want to become a shaman (or a *chomchaengi*), but if I don't do this, I would die." In brief, the contribution of shamans and *chomchaengi* to society is verbally not heralded (except in a few instances) nor is it rewarded by high social rank or position, though some achieve financial recognition. Yes, a few shamans (not *chomchaengi*) now are honored as exponents of Korea's true religion, but for each one this famous there are many who earn a reasonable living and the devotion of their clients, all the while being condemned by society at large as low class, dishonest, and hopelessly backward swindlers. It's complicated, of course, and not testable, but perhaps this double bind—utilized but scorned, sought but socially separated, touted individually but disparaged as a group—has contributed to their power. The tradition of simultaneous fear and loathing/hope and trust puts shamans and *chomchaengi* in a double bind which, analogous to similar communication patterns in families, suspends them in a marginal or ambivalent position vis-a-vis society.[9] As outsiders who have an intimate cultural understanding, shamans and *chomchaengi* are in an excellent position to be participant-observers: they may not write ethnographies but their marginality may give them a distance and self-consciousness integral to their advice, inspirations, and interpretations. It may also give them a certain fascination in the eyes of clients. Clients frequently cite the spiritual experiences of *chomchaengi* (as well as a friend's recommendation) as their virtue, but undoubtedly their existence on the periphery of the social order has some attraction. As I.M. Lewis has noted, it is not difficult to see in spirit possession an oblique outcry against social injustices, and for clients suffering the hardships of family life and city life, counsel by someone who has partially stepped out of the system (or intermittently does so) may be just the antidote to depression, worry or discontent.[10] Of course, this puts me in a bit of a double bind myself. Having met so many *chomchaengi* who experienced hardships on their way to becoming diviners and who suffer low status because of their occupation, I find it uncomfortable to stand by and assert that low status is a necessary price for genius. It seems likely, however, that in both a sociological and a psychological sense, the spiritual power of shamans and *chomchaengi* and their marginal status are not unrelated. Having said at the outset that *chomchaengi* do a thriving business *despite* their problematical status, I must now suggest that in future research we explore the possibility that *chomchaengi* do a flourishing business partly *because* of their marginal status. It seems to me that the appeal of stepping outside the boundaries of approved rational analysis, if only for a moment, ought not to be discounted.

Future is as Future Does

If my characterization of Korea's lady fortunetellers as practically the shamans of the future has done nothing but introduce them to you as a good way to spend some time during your next trip to Seoul, I will be pleased. In fact, I wholeheartedly recommend *chomchaengi,* however you wish to categorize them, for your future consideration. They seem to exhibit the compelling combination of a divination style similar to shamans, a function like that of counsellors or psychotherapists, the features of a female professional class, and a status in society which is low and marginal, but not completely powerless. In sum, I hope the mysterious woman in your future is a *chomchaengi*.

Notes

1. My observations are based on fieldwork done in Seoul during the summer of 1975 and from June 1976 to September 1977 and on archival research through January 1978 funded by a travel grant from the Department of Anthropology, University of Washington; a Fulbright-Hays Dissertation Grant; and a grant (PHS-NIH-MH-05896-01) from the National Institute of Mental Health, for each of which I am very grateful. Innumerable individuals in Korea and the United States have aided my efforts, and I greatly appreciate their contributions. Any mistakes in this paper are, of course, my own.

2. Although *"chomjaengi"* would be a closer approximation of the pronunciation of this word, I have retained the spelling *"chomchaengi"* because of its existence in the English literature on Korea.

3. For an accurate and evocative description of one kind of shaman ceremony *(kut),* see Kendall 1977a.

4. Lunar years are counted in cycles of sixty in which each unit (of sixty) is marked with two characters, one of the Ten Heavenly Stems and the other one of the Twelve Earthly Branches. This same cycle is also applied to lunar months, days, and two-hour periods. The eight characters which identify one's birthdate (a Stem and a Branch character for the year, month, day and hour of birth), known as *"sajup'alcha"* (the four pillars and the eight characters), can be used to divine one's future.

5. For a description in English of urban shamans and their activities, see Kim T. G. 1978.

6. For a description in English of divination techniques of Korean shamans, see Lee J. Y. 1976.

7. Research on how women become shamans, including case histories, is reported in Harvey 1976.

8. I.M. Lewis, *Ecstatic Religion: An Anthropological Study of Spirit Possession and Shamanism* (Middlesex, England: Pelican Books, 1971), pp. 100-126.

9. G. Bateson, *Steps to an Ecology of Mind* (New York: Chandler Publishing Co., 1972), pp. 206-216.

10. Lewis, *op. cit.,* pp. 127-148.

Bibliography

Bateson, Gregory. *Steps to an Ecology of Mind.* New York: Chandler Publishing Co. 1972.

Chang Chu-Gun. *Kyonggido Ch'iyok Musok* (Shaman Practices of Kyonggido Province). Seoul: Ministry of Culture. 1967.

Chang Chu-Gun and Choi Gil-Song. *"Mingan Sinang"* (Popular Beliefs) in D. H. Lee, C. G. Chang, and K. K. Lee (Eds.), *Hanguk Minsokhak Kaesol* (Introduction to Korean Folklore), pp. 128-196. Seoul: Minjung Sawongwan. 1974.

Harvey, Young-Sook Kim. *Korean Mudang: Socialization Experiences of Six Female Shamans.* Honolulu: University of Hawaii (Doctoral Dissertation). 1976.

Janelli, Dawnhee Yim. *Logical Contradictions in Korean Learned Fortunetelling: A Dissertation in Folklore and Folklife.* Philadelphia: University of Pennsylvania (Doctoral Dissertation). 1977.

Kendall, Laurel. "Caught Between Ancestors and Spirits: Field Report of a Korean *Mansin's* Healing *Kut,*" *Korea Journal* 17 (8): 8-23. 1977a.

"*Mugam:* The Dance in Shaman's Clothing," *Korea Journal* 17(12): 38-44. 1977b.

Kim Tae-Gon. "Shamanism in the Seoul Area," *Korea Journal* 18(6): 39-51. 1978.

Kim Yung-Chung (Ed.). *Women of Korea: A History from Ancient Times to 1945* (Abridged and translated version of *Han'guk Yosong-sa*). Seoul: Ewha Womans University. 1976.

Kinsler, Arthur W. *A Study in Fertility Cult for Children in Korean Shamanism.* Seoul: Yonsei University (Doctoral Dissertation). 1976.

Lee, Jung-Young. "Divination in Korean Shamanistic Thought," *Korea Journal* 16 (11): 5-11. 1976.

Lewis, I.M. *Ecstatic Religion: An Anthropological Study of Spirit Possession and Shamanism.* Middlesex, England: Pelican Books. 1971.

Turner, Victor. *The Forest of Symbols.* Ithaca: Cornell University Press. 1967

Yi Nung-Hwa; "Choson Musok-Ko" (A Study of Korean Shamanism), *Kemyong* 19:1-85. 1927.

8 / A Kut For The Chon Family

LAUREL KENDALL

When the god of the roofbeam is out of sorts,
The master of the house is out of sorts.
When the god of the foundation is out of sorts,
The lady of the house is out of sorts.
— a Kyonggi shaman chant

Clanging cymbals and the steady thump of an hour-glass drum draw women and children to the gateway of a Korean house. They know from the flood of sound in the alleyway that shamans are doing a *kut,* and a *kut* is high entertainment. The gods appear throughout the night in the person of the costumed shaman. The ancestors arrive and the family cries for the dead. There is music, dance and song. There are moments of high drama and comedy.

The *kut* for the Chon family was one of more than forty such rituals I saw during a year and a half of field work. I followed after the shaman "Yongsu's Mother" when she performed *kut.* The shaman would explain my presence, "This one is a student; they sent her from America to study this sort of thing."

What follows is a frankly flamboyant description of a flamboyant event. I will let the action of the *kut* speak for itself, with a minimum of introductory remarks to set the stage and introduce the players.

In the northern half of the Korean peninsula one politely addresses a shaman as *"mansin."* The name means "ten-thousand gods," for the shaman is a recognized professional practitioner who manifests the gods in her own person at will. She interprets the visions they send her, and importunes them on behalf of the women who seek her aid.

Korean friends in Seoul have told me that shamans were a part of Korean life long ago, that a few might yet be found in the deep country. In fact, the sound of the *mansin's* drum along city alleyways belies this assumption. Cosmopolitan Koreans consider shamanism the romantic relic of a distant past. Shaman dances performed in Seoul's National Theatre draw a mixed crowd of curious young intellectuals who approach the event as entertainment and remain in their seats, and women in traditional dress who approach the stage and bow before the shaman's blades. In many houses in both city and country, among both rich and poor, the shaman remains an acknowledged ritual expert and a recourse in crisis.

The Seoul Metropolitan Government reports that in 1975 there were 902 shamans practicing in the city of Seoul. Since this figure includes only shamans acknowledged in the records of the district office and village chief, the actual number is far higher. According to the Economic Planning Board, there were 6,040 shamans in the entire country in 1963, or roughly one shaman for each 750 households, but again, the count is far below the actual number of practicing shamans.[1] These figures do not include inspirational diviners *(chom chaengi)* who, like the shamans, interpret visions for clients after an initial inspirational calling. The inspirational diviner does not perform rituals to placate the gods and ancestors. For this, the inspirational diviner refers a client to a shaman.

In the villages north of Seoul, where I did field work, a woman is never more than a ten-minutes bus ride away from a shaman when she needs a divination or an exorcism. When village households do *kut,* women gather. The *mansin* is more than a curiosity here. She is the woman's ritual specialist.

Among her many tasks, she exorcises ghosts, fumigates wood imps from the house, and leads the dead to paradise. A woman becomes a shaman through a traumatic possession sickness, initiation, and apprenticeship to a more experienced *mansin.*

In descriptions of Korea, the shaman is called *"mudang."* In direct address, the term is derogatory. I use the more polite and localized term *"mansin,"* the term I used to address the shamans I knew. Hereditary priestesses in the southern provinces are also called *mudang,* but they are not shamans. By virtue of birth in a family of priests and musicians, and trained from childhood, they address the gods with song and dance. They do not experience divine possession, neither initially nor when they perform rituals, and they receive no visions.

The shaman is almost always a woman. Male shamans, *paksu,* are rare, although a few are active in Seoul and the surrounding countryside. I met two during my fieldwork.

Mansin are known by professional nicknames, "The Chatterbox *Mansin,"* "the Boil-face *Mansin,"* "the Brass Mirror

Mansin," or by location, "The Clear Spring *Mansin,"* "The Town *Mansin."* By Korean etiquette, an adult is rarely if ever called by a given name. Village women are known as the mothers of village children, Yongsu's Mother, Okkyong's Mother. I use these "baby-mother" *(aegioma)* titles for the *mansin* and village women I knew best. A woman is sometimes known by where she lives, "The Tile-roof Auntie," "The Hilltop Auntie," or by what she does, "The Noodle Shop Auntie," the "Rice Shop Auntie." Any woman is politely an "aunt" or a "grandmother," depending on her age.

The Korean wife is also called "house person" *(chip saram)* or "the one inside" *(anae).* The house is set and setting for the *kut* the *mansin* performs at the housewife's request. For the Chon family *kut,* one must imagine a traditional Korean country house. There are two hot floor rooms heated with charcoal in the flues underneath. A broad wooden porch separates the two rooms. A low-roofed kitchen, store rooms, and stock pens are all built around a mud courtyard. An elevated platform at the side of the house holds earthen storage jars of soy sauce and pepper paste. Low walls conceal the low building from the village lane, but the great front gate is open to the fields.

This is the Chon house.

Dramitis Personae

The Shamans
The Chatterbox *Mansin*—Grandmother Chon's regular shaman; she organized the kut.
Okkyong's Mother—The Chatterbox *Mansin's* apprentice "spirit daughter."
Yongsu's Mother
The Town *Mansin*

The Household
Grandfather Chon—old man whose illness is the primary reason for this *kut.*
Grandmother Chon—Grandfather Chon's second wife.

The Family
The son—Grandfather Chon's child by his first wife.
The daughter-in-law—the son's wife.
Their children—Grandfather and Grandmother Chon's grandchildren.

The kindred
The daughter—Grandfather Chon's married daughter by his first wife.
The maternal aunt—Grandmother Chon's own sister.
The sister-in-law—Grandfather Chon's sister.

The women
The friend—Grandmother Chon's friend from her natal village, the sister-in-law's neighbor.
Women who live in the Chons' neighborhood.

The ancestors
Parents—Grandfather Chon's father and mother, father-in-law and mother-in-law to Grandmother Chon.
Wife—Grandfather Chon's first wife, mother of the son and daughter.

Preliminaries

The cold November sun fades over rooftops of slate, straw and corrugated metal. Shadows lengthen in fields of rice stubble. There is a bustle of activity behind the Chon house wall: the clatter of incessant chopping in the kitchen and the rise and fall of many voices in the hot floor inner room. Women emerge from the kitchen with steaming tubs of rice cake. The Chatterbox *Mansin* shrills out directions, telling the women how to arrange offerings for the household spirits. The Chon family is holding a *kut* to cure Grandfather Chon of a nagging illness.

About a month ago, Grandfather Chon went on an outing with his cronies. This carousing precipitated an upset stomach. The upset stomach developed into a general state of malaise. Grandmother Chon described Grandfather Chon's complaint to the pharmacist in town and brought home the pharmacist's preparation: several packets each containing five colored pills in white powder. When this treatment brought no relief, Grandfather Chon went to an outpatient clinic for the standard treatment, an unspecified shot. An expensive series of shots brought no marked change in Grandfather Chon's condition. Now Grandmother Chon went to the Chatterbox *Mansin,* a shaman she has consulted for several years, and received a divination.

As Grandmother Chon suspected, her Great Spirit Grandmother (*Taesin Halmoni*) was greedy for a *kut*. A dead shaman influences the affairs of her descendants as the Great Spirit Grandmother of their household pantheon. An active Great Spirit Grandmother bestows blessings and protection on the family, but every three years or so, she must be feasted and entertained with a *kut*. The Chons hadn't held a *kut* now for five or six years. Grandfather Chon's illness is a warning. The ritual is overdue and further misfortune might follow more delay.

Although Grandfather Chon was dangerously ill some weeks ago, he is now able to lounge about in pajamas, chatting with friends who drop by. He is a small, light-framed man with white hair and a neatly clipped beard. Grandmother Chon is a lean woman, bent with arthritis, but lively and quick to smile.

The Chons live alone, fairly comfortably, raising pigs and rabbits. The hot floor rooms are freshly papered and well-furnished with chests and cabinets. A large television stands in the main hot floor room. Color reproductions of traditional folk paintings cut from a calendar decorate one wall.

The Chons' son and his wife live in Seoul where the son is trying his luck, not very successfully, as a shopkeeper. Son, daughter-in-law, and grandchildren returned today for the *kut*. The Chons' married daughter also returned. Grandmother Chon's own sister is here from Seoul, a plump woman with short grey hair wearing a ready-made trouser suit. She beams, happily anticipating *kut* festivities. Grandfather Chon's sister arrives with one of Grandmother Chon's old friends from her natal village. Both of these women are wearing fancy Korean dresses shot with silver thread; a *kut* is a special occasion.

Four *mansin* will perform the *kut*. Because Grandmother Chon is the Chatterbox *Mansin's* own client, the Chatterbox *Mansin* is in charge. She has brought along her own apprentice "spirit daughter" *(sinttal)*, Okkyong's Mother, although Okkyong's Mother is not yet trained to do much besides hitting the cymbals. She has also brought Yongsu's Mother and Town *Mansin*. The Town *Mansin* seldom performs *kut* for fear of embarrassing her married daughter, but she is an old acquaintance of the Chon family. When the Chatterbox *Mansin* invited her, she agreed to perform this *kut*.

The Kut Begins

In the last of the afternoon light, the *mansin* carry the hour-glass drum, mats, and a tray of wine and rice cake offerings out the gate to the flat space in front of the Chon house wall. A few women from the neighborhood gather in front of the house; more will drift over once the drumming starts.

The *mansin* yell for everyone to come out of the house. Women emerge, red-faced from the kitchen. Grandfather Chon, bundled up in an overcoat against the wind, hobbles out and sits far off to the left of the drum with a couple of his friends. The women crowd close together around the drum. Children wander about between the women's skirts. At the start of a *kut,* no one can remain inside the house, and everyone must stand wide of the overhanging roof. Women even lead cows and dogs outside the enclosed courtyard before the drumming starts. When the *mansin* first hits the drum, the household gods open wide their eyes. This is a dangerous moment; like the geni imprisoned in the bottle, awakened household gods seize upon whatever greets their gaze.

Yongsu's Mother hits the drum. Okkyong's Mother hits the cymbals. The Chatterbox *Mansin* declares before the gods and ancestors that the Chon family is holding a *kut.* The *mansin* drive unclean, noxious influences away from the house. They invite gods from mountains and distant places to enter the house and be entertained.

The Chatterbox *Mansin* takes a long blue vest from the top of the drum. She dances, pumping her arms up and down, jumping on the balls of her feet. She stops, scowling at the offering tray. She flings wide her vest and hisses: "There is a Great Spirit in this house, there is, there is."

This is the first appearance of the greedy spirit Officials (*Taegam*). The Officials make trouble when they see wealth—money and possessions—going into the house. The family should share their good fortune; give the Officials a cup of wine. This particular Official is the Soldier (*Kunung Taegam*), one of the worst. The Soldier Official prowls outside the house wall, spying on the family. He is particularly dangerous because he travels about with the Death Messenger (*Saja*).

The Soldier Official chides Grandmother Chon for past neglect and for the paucity of her offerings. No supernatural Official is ever satisfied with the offerings. Grandmother Chon promises more and better food later if the Official will make her husband well. This exchange is stereotypic, repeated throughout this and other *kut.* Grandmother Chon knows her part. If she didn't, Yongsu's Mother and Okkyong's Mother would coach her from the drum or importune the god on her behalf.

With another burst of drumming and dance, the Chatterbox *Mansin* removes her costume. She breaks the head off the fish with her foot, and flings it into the fields. She throws scraps of food from the offering table and cupfuls of wine after the fish head, thus bidding all greedy Officials, ghosts, and noxious influences to eat, drink, and depart. The *mansin* flings down the fish. The decapitated trunk points inward, toward the open gate of the house. Quickly, she pours and tosses more cups of wine. Again, she casts down the fish. The trunk points out, toward the fields. This first batch of spirits is satisfied.

Yongsu's Mother, still hitting the drum, walks through the gate and into the courtyard. The women all follow her. She sets the drum on the edge of the wooden porch between the two hot floor rooms and continues to play while Okkyong's Mother hits the cymbals at her side. The process of the *kut* is now within the walls of the house.

Rites Within the Walls

The *mansin* and the Chon family eat a hasty meal. The Chatterbox *Mansin* performs a drum song on the porch. She sits before the two offering tables, one for the household gods and one for the ancestors, both piled high with fruit, rice cake, fried fish, pickled vegetables, nuts, and candy. The drum song lasts a full forty-five minutes. The *mansin* sings out the names and ages of all of the family members, announcing them to the gods. She includes the married son, daughter-in-law, and grandchildren, although they live in a separate household, but she leaves out the daughter, married into another family. By singing the first segment of the song, the *mansin* expels pollutions *(pujong)* accumulated in the house through birth, death and time since the last ritual cleansing. Halfway through the song, Yongsu's Mother fills two dippers with water. Into the first she puts three pinches of ash, three pinches of red pepper powder, and three pinches of salt. This is "pollution water:" ash and water are a traditional soap base, salt and red pepper are used in exorcism. Yongsu's Mother waves the dippers over the offering tables, then through the hot floor inner room. The house is clean.

The Chatterbox *Mansin* now sings long lists of household

gods, major and minor, inviting them to enter the house. Grand-mother Chon lights the candles on the offering trays, sets down two thousand-won bills, and bows with her head to the floor. She bows a full dozen bows.

The Chatterbox *Mansin* finishes her song and smokes a cigarette before she begins the next segment of the *kut*.

The next sequence is for the Chon family's ancestors, but several gods appear first, leading the ancestors back to the house. Each category of god has a special costume. The Chatterbox *Man-sin*, in a jade green robe, manifests accumulated distant dead *(sop-su)*, who appear but briefly. The Chatterbox *Mansin* waves her tassled exorcism wands over the offering tables and over the heads of the family members in the hot floor room. She flings down the exorcism wands. They point out toward the open courtyard. The distant dead are satisfied; their influence is gone.

Now the Chatterbox *Mansin* puts on a broad-sleeved red robe over the green robe. She carries a high-crowned red hat. The most regal gods in the pantheon wear this costume as kings or magistrates. Facing the open courtyard, she holds a paper fan open wide in front of her face. The drum plays as her lips form a silent invocation. The fan trembles, the drum picks up speed, and the *mansin* waves the fan, dancing in time. This is the Mountain God of the Chon family's ancestral home (Ponhyang Sansin). When this deity is satisfied, the dead are pacified under the Mountain God's rule. When the family neglects offerings or when the Mountain God is affronted by pollution, he drops his guard and lets the ancestors move among the living, bringing sickness and misfor-tune.

The Mountain God chides Grandmother Chon for neglect. Grandmother Chon spreads a bill on the Mountain God's open fan. The Mountain God tells her, "Don't worry, Lady Chon, I will make your husband well. I will make you rich. I will help your son become rich. I will help your grandchildren speak well and write well."

The Chatterbox *Mansin* removes the red robe revealing the green robe again underneath. Twelve suicides who serve as nether-worldly guards *(kamang)* make a brief appearance. Grandmother Chon places another bill on the *mansin's* fan.

Now the Chatterbox *Mansin* puts on a yellow robe for the

Great Spirit Grandmother, the god who will lead the Chon family ancestors into the home. This is the powerful and angry god most directly responsible for Grandfather Chon's illness. The Great Spirit Grandmother picks up the *mansin's* huge battle fork and broad sword and jabs at the tub of rice cake the family prepared for her. She indicates, with a raised gesture of the arm, what a huge pile of rice cake it would take to satisfy her. She grabs the married daughter and drags her up to the wooden porch where the daughter bows before the offering trays. The Great Spirit Grandmother berates Grandmother Chon for preparing such a small amount of rice cake. Grandmother Chon yells, "Then make us rich, and next time we'll give you more." The Great Spirit Grandmother asks for a new yellow robe. She fingers Grandmother Chon's crumpled skirt and complains, "Your clothes are much nicer than mine." Grandmother Chon sputters, "What do you mean, better than yours?" Yongsu's Mother chimes in from behind the drum, "Yes, grandmother, your skirt is much nicer." Grandmother Chon continues to protest. The Great Spirit Grandmother offers her fan to the daughter who puts a five-hundred won bill on it demanding, "Make us all rich." The deity offers her fan to the plump daughter-in-law who giggles her protest, "I'm not surnamed Chon." But the Great Spirit Grandmother persists and the daughter-in-law contributes.

The Great Spirit Grandmother enters the inner room and demands money from Grandfather Chon. Grandfather Chon looks confused. Grandmother Chon bursts in yelling, "How do you expect a sick person to have any money on him?" She puts another bill on the Great Spirit Grandmother's fan. Okkyong's Mother pleads on behalf of the Chons, "Please, Great Spirit Grandmother, make Grandfather Chon well." The Great Spirit Grandmother smiles and tells Grandfather Chon, "You've given me this money, so I'll make you well. Don't worry, old man, you're not going to die. Now just give me one of these (she indicates her yellow robe), and I'll be quiet." She sings a song praising herself as a "good and wonderful Great Spirit Grandmother."

The ancestors appear next, sobbing "*Aigo, aigo.*" Grandfather Chon, wrapped in a blanket, sits facing the wall. He doesn't want to participate. The Chatterbox *Mansin* turns to Grandmother Chon, clutches her shoulders, and weeps. The *mansin* manifests

mother-in-law and father-in-law. The neighbor women demand of
the ancestors, "Why have you made your own son sick? Please,
please make him well." The parental ancestors promise help. "Will
he live past ninety, then?" Grandmother Chon asks the manifestation of her mother-in-law. "Ninety, that's too long," says the
ancestor. There is laughter. "Past eighty, then?" "That may be
possible, and I'll do well by my grandchildren."

The next ancestor weeps yet more violently, "Why did I die
early; why did I die before my time?" Grandmother Chon says
bluntly, "Well then, why did you go and die?" The ancestor turns
to weep over the daughter and Grandmother Chon informs the anthropologist, "This is my husband's first wife. She died in
childbirth." The ancestor takes the five-hundred-won bill that
Grandmother Chon holds out.

The much anticipated Official's sequence is next. Yongsu's
Mother dances as the Official. Her sharp-tongued humor is well-
suited to the portrayal of a greedy supernatural Official. In a blue
vest and broad-brimmed black hat, the basic costume of palace
guards and low-level functionaries in historic films and television
dramas set in the last two centuries, she dances vigorously. Suddenly, unpredictably, she grabs the Mountain God's red robe from the
clothesline. The Chatterbox *Mansin,* from behind the drum,
gestures toward the yellow robe, "This one, this one." Yongsu's
Mother grabs the yellow robe and waves both costumes through the
air. She throws down the red robe and puts on the yellow robe. The
Great Spirit Official of the Chon family has come to the *kut* along
with the family's various other Officials.

The Official grabs Grandmother Chon by the ears and drags
her over to the center of the porch. Grandmother Chon again protests that her own clothes aren't nearly so nice as the yellow spirit
robe. The Chatterbox *Mansin* contradicts her from the sidelines.
"No, Grandmother, yours are ever so much nicer." The *mansin*
and gods are still insisting that the Chons provide a new yellow
robe.

Yongsu's Mother continues to manifest the Official in pan-
tomine. She sticks a finger in her ear, twists it, and scowls; the
Chons should have hired a musician to play the flute and fiddle for
the Official's pleasure. The god pulls Grandmother Chon to the
Official's rice cake steamer and glares at the two pig's legs piled on

top. The Official smears Grandmother Chon's face with grease from the pig's legs. Grandmother Chon hands the Official a bill. The Official wipes his nose with it, then casts the crumpled banknote at the drummer who stuffs it in the collection bag tied to the drum. The Official spreads wide his arms indicating the height of a pile of delicacies that would satisfy his appetite.

The Official hobbles on all fours; the Official wants a whole pig. The Official limps, balancing on the two short pig's legs; the Official wants two big legs from a cow.

By now, the two hot floor rooms and the edges of the porch are full of women. They giggle at the Official's antics as they pass kettles of wine.

The Official drags the son onto the porch and shakes the long ribbons that fasten the yellow robe into all of his pockets. The Official pours a cup of wine to give the young man luck. The maternal aunt capers around the porch. She waves a bill in her hand as she dances, teasing the Official. The Official pulls the maternal aunt's clothing away from her back and fans up inside with the hems of her costume, dusting the maternal aunt with auspicious forces. The Official claims money from the maternal aunt, cackling the Official's characteristic laugh, "Ahahaha!"

The Official grabs the daughter-in-law and gives her a dusting of luck with the fan. The daughter-in-law draws out a five-hundred-won bill from her pocket. The Official backs away, disdainful of the small amount. The daughter-in-law hesitantly draws out her coin purse. The Official tries to look inside. The Official pours cups of wine for the daughter-in-law and the daughter, then demands more money. "Must I give you my return bus fare?" asks the daughter-in-law, holding out one of the new Seoul bus tokens. Everyone laughs. The Official is indignant, "I'd have to go to Seoul to spend that."

The Official holds out the pig's legs, indicating that the women must stuff bills between the hooves. The maternal aunt tries to stuff in another bus token, but the Official jerks the hoof away. Grandmother Chon holds out her skirt and receives both pig's legs in her lap. While the drumming continues, the Official gestures for a towel, and twists it into a head pad. Women hoist the tub of rice cake, pig's legs on top, to the *mansin's* padded head. In her own voice, Yongsu's Mother calls to the Chatterbox *Mansin,* "Give me my rubber shoes."

The Chatterbox *Mansin* tosses the shoes down to the ground below the porch. The drummer strikes a rapid rhythm. The Official circles the courtyard, followed by Grandmother Chon who carries a huge kettle of wine. The Official flings cups of wine in all of the corners of the courtyard, in the store rooms, the rabbit hutches, and the pig stye. The Official circles around the house within the wall, past the platform where the family keeps jars of soy and pepper paste, around the back of the house, and back to the porch, all the while spilling cups of wine. Throughout the Official's progress, Yongsu's Mother gracefully balances some thirty pounds of rice cake, meat, and terra-cotta on her head. She flings down the empty wine cup and passes the tub of rice cake backwards over her head to Grandmother Chon who receives it standing on the porch.

Back on the porch with hat in place, the Official indicates that Grandmother Chon must place bills under the crown of the hat and under the chin band at the cheeks. When only the chin remains empty of bills, the Official snatches the next bill from Grandmother Chon and puts it under the chest band. The Official again points to the empty chin, asking Grandmother Chon for one more bill. But the next bill is snatched for the chest band. The Official sticks the next two bills behind her back, securing them under the chest band. The Official laughs. The women laugh. The Official finally secures a bill under the chin.

The Official sells wine to Grandmother Chon, the son, the maternal aunt, the paternal aunt, the daughter-in-law, and the daughter. Singing the Official's song, "Such a wonderful Official I am, so wonderful I just can't say," the Official sells cups of wine to the women in the hot floor rooms who return the empty cups with small coins. Grandmother Chon follows behind the Official with a plate of soy-salted fish and a pair of chopsticks; a bite of food should follow a cup of wine. The drumming goes on and out on the porch, the maternal aunt continues to dance.

The Official divines the next year, advising caution for the early months and improved fortunes in the late spring. Yongsu's mother removes her hat and vest and passes the costume to the son's outstreched arms. "You've put yourself out," Grandmother Chon tells Yongsu's Mother. "What do you mean, put myself out?" Yongsu's mother makes a polite disclaimer.

There is a long pause in the *kut*. Members of the family and other women will "use the *mugam*." One by one, they put on the *mansin's* costumes and dance before the drum. The *mansin* claim that good luck follows upon entertaining one's personal Body-governing God (*Momju*) by dancing in the costume appropriate to the god. When the woman dances, her personal god ascends and dances. When the god is satisfied, the woman and her family have good fortune. Women attest to the sheer pleasure of *mugam* dancing.[2]

In a healing *kut*, like the Chon family *kut*, the patient must dance in costume and appease his or her Body-governing God. When the patient is a man, particularly a venerable older man, he is usually reluctant to engage in abandoned public display. He must be coaxed. The Chatterbox *Mansin* persuades Grandfather Chon to dance, then leads him out to the porch. The *mansin* clothe Grandfather Chon in the white monk's robe and peaked cowl because the women in the Chon family pray to the Seven Stars (*Ch'ilsong*) for the birth and health of sons. They wear the Seven Stars' white robe when they dance *mugam* and their own Body-governing Seven Stars ascends.

The Chatterbox *mansin* coaches Grandfather Chon by dancing in front of him to show him how. She grabs his wrists and moves his arms to the music. He smiles ever so slightly, but then drops his arms, proclaiming his inability to dance. He returns to the inner room. Grandmother Chon dances next in the Great Spirit Grandmother's yellow robe. The maternal aunt dances at her side. Grandmother Chon is soon rapidly jumping before the drum; her personal Great Spirit has "ascended."

The *mansin* call out the daughter-in-law next. She demurs saying, "You have to know how to dance." Grandmother Chon yells at her, "Get out there and dance. It'll bring you luck." The daughter-in-law's luck is the luck of the son's household. The *mansin* dress her in the white robe of the Seven Stars. As she dances, faster and faster, the Chatterbox *Mansin* throws the yellow robe over the white costume. The Chatterbox *Mansin* discerns the influence of two personal deities, the Great Spirit and the Seven Stars. The daughter-in-law dances to a frenzy. Okkyong's Mother stands beside the dancing woman, beating the rhythm on cymbals, tapping her foot in time, and nodding encouragement. The daughter-in-law finally collapses in a bow before the offering table.

The women in the hot floor rooms nod consensus, "The god ascended. Yes, the god ascended." (*sini ollatta*).

The *mansin* call the daughter to dance. Like the daughter-in-law, she claims that she doesn't know how. The Chatterbox *Mansin* holds out the white robe. From the two hot floor rooms, the women shout, "Dance and you'll have luck; wear that and you'll look pretty." The daughter, too, goes from a graceful dance to vigorous jumping which she sustains for several minutes. The Town *Mansin* relieves Okkyong's Mother on the cymbals. The daughter jumps precariously close to the edge of the porch, but the maternal aunt stands below the edge, arms held wide, to protect the daughter from falling. When the daughter is finished, the women tease her, "And you said you couldn't dance."

Now the maternal aunt dances in the blue vest of the Official. The Chatterbox *Mansin* encourages her to put on the Great Spirit Grandmother's yellow robe. The maternal aunt refuses. Though she dances gracefully and with a distant smile on her lips, she can't seem to reach the point of ecstatic jumping. The Chatterbox *Mansin* again urges her to put on the yellow robe. Thus attired, the maternal aunt begins, almost immediately, to jump. The maternal aunt stamps her feet and pounds her arms at the air. For the *mansin,* this behavior indicates a strong, greedy, demanding personal spirit. Thus, the maternal aunt siezes any opportunity to dance, and plunges into the action of the *kut.*

Grandmother Chon's sister-in-law dances next, followed by the friend from Grandmother Chon's native place. Thirteen neighbor women and the anthropologist use the *mugam.* I recognize some of these women from other *kut,* and they recognize me. A few of them danced at the Chatterbox *Mansin's* annual *kut* for the spirits of her own shrine early in the Fall.

It is well past midnight when the women finish dancing. Many of the women leave now. Yongsu's Mother shouts for food. The *mansin,* family, and lingering guests eat rice and hot soup.

The Chatterbox *Mansin* realizes that they have forgotten the segment for the Buddhist Sage (*Pulsa*), normally performed early in the *kut.* They have reached the point where they can perform the segment for the Birth Grandmother in the inner room (*Chesok*).[3] Since the Birth Grandmother, the Buddhist Sage, and the Seven Stars are all Buddhist spirits concerned with birth and children, the

Chatterbox *Mansin* sees no harm in combining these gods in a single segment. She gives final instructions to her "spirit daughter," Okkyong's Mother, who will perform this segment. Since the Buddhist Sage and the Birth Grandmother are considered relatively easy gods to manifest, *mansin* usually begin performing *kut* with these segments, but Okkyong's Mother still requires some coaching. On the porch, Okkyong's Mother invokes all of the various varieties of Buddhist Sage. She grabs the cymbals from the Town *Mansin* and performs a rapid dance to signify possession. She puts on her shoes and runs to the side of the house where the women have set offerings of rice cake, water, and burning candles on the tall earthenware storage jars. This is where the Chon women worship the Seven Stars. Grandmother Chon, the maternal aunt, the daughter, the daughter-in-law, and a small knot of women gather, rubbing their hands and bowing while Okkyong's Mother invokes the Seven Stars. She performs a quick divination for Grandmother Chon, then rushes back to the inner room where a special tray of vegetarian offerings — rice cake, fruit, and nuts — awaits the Birth Grandmother. Like all deities, the Birth Grandmother denounces the poor quality of offering food and the delay between rituals. Then, the Birth Grandmother promises aid. With her cymbals, Okkyong's Mother scoops nuts and dates from the offering tray and flips them into Grandmother Chon's outstretched skirt. Okkyong's Mother fingers the nuts and candies, divining for the son, "Someone will help him with his business. For the next two months, he should be cautious in human relations and not make any decisive move. In the second or third month of next year, there will be good news."

Okkyong's Mother gives a divination for each of the grandchildren as she tosses more nuts and candy into Grandmother Chon's skirt. Grandmother Chon gives the name and age of each grandchild, and Okkyong's Mother incorporates this information into her chant. Grandmother Chon isn't sure of the age of one of her grandchildren and confers with the daughter-in-law before Okkyong's Mother can continue chanting.

Okkyong's Mother removes the peaked cowl while dancing and begins to remove the white robe. The Chatterbox *Mansin* and Yong-su's Mother shout to Okkyong's Mother that she has forgotten to invoke the unredeemed souls in the Buddhist hell (*chonan*).

Okkyong's Mother begins to replace the cowl but the Chatterbox *Mansin* tells her it isn't necessary. The apprentice *mansin* quickly invokes the list of unredeemed souls.

Now Okkyong's Mother removes the white robe. She throws the red nylon skirt of her costume over her head and holds it out wide with an open fan in front of her face. She manifests the Princess *(Hogu),* a capricious dead maiden who causes domestic strife. The Princess says, "I go flutter, flutter, flutter in the inner room." The Princess is paid off with a five-hundred-won bill and departs.

The Chatterbox *Mansin* dresses in three layers of robes for the war gods who will appear next. Yongsu's Mother coaches Okkyong's Mother in the invocation for the unredeemed souls, since Okkyong's Mother botched the order of the chant. The Chatterbox *Mansin* realizes that Okkyong's Mother forgot to sell nuts and candies from the Birth Grandmother's offering tray. She tells her to do it now. Singing, Okkyong's Mother circulates through the rooms spilling sweets into the laps of the women who place small coins on the cymbals she carries. The older women know the song and laughing, sing along, "Eat a date and give birth to a daughter, eat a chestnut and give birth to a son." They stuff nuts and candies into pockets and nibble them during the *kut* or hoard them for a favorite grandchild at home. Like drinking wine purchased from the Official and dancing the *mugam,* the women gain fortune when they purchase and consume these sweets from the cymbals.

Now the war gods appear, manifested by the Chatterbox *Mansin.* The General *(Changgun)* is first in a wide-sleeved blue robe and high-crowned hat, striding majestically to the processional cadence of cymbals. The *mansin* say that the General and the Mountain Spirit are like kings. You give them money first without their even asking. The General is above the greedy, demanding antics of the Official. The General is followed by the Special Messenger *(Pyolsang),*[4] in a black jacket with red sleeves and a broad-brimmed black hat. The Special Messenger wields the broad sword and battle fork. The Chatterbox *Mansin* balances the sword on an overturned saucer. She jabs pigs legs onto the prongs of the battle fork and tries to balance this unwieldy object. Balancing the meat is a moment of some tension. If the trident stands on its own, the household gods have accepted the *kut* offering. If the battlefork continues to wobble in the *mansin's* hands, the gods are unsatisfied and it bodes no good for the family. The Chatterbox *Mansin* calls for salt and pours it on the saucer for traction. Grandmother Chon sets two five-hundred-won bills on top of the meat and rubs her hands in supplication. The battle fork stands. The Chatterbox *Mansin* sings the praises of the Special Messenger as she circulates cups of wine around the handle of the upright battle fork and passes them to Grandmother Chon, the daughter-in-law and the daughter. They return each cup with a small coin on the saucer rim. Like the wine the Official sold, this is also "lucky wine."

Now the Warrior (*Sinjang*) appears. Ghosts and other noxious influences fear the knife the Warrior wields. The spirit Warrior will exorcise Grandfather Chon. Okkyong's Mother whispers that Grandfather Chon has already gone to sleep in the inner room. Yongsu's Mother says they'll just have Grandfather Chon appear quickly on the porch and he can go right back to sleep. Grandmother Chon leads Grandfather Chon out to the end of the porch where the *mansin* ask him to kneel, facing the court-yard. The *mansin* cover him with a strip of thin yellow cloth, an offering to wandering ghosts, one of his own shirts, and the Warrior's five-colored divination flags. They prop the huge battle fork and sword on either side of his body.

Yong-su's Mother kneels beside Grandfather Chon, banging the cymbals in close proximity to his right ear. With a series of whoops, the Chatterbox *Mansin* pelts Grandfather Chon's covered form with handfuls of millet. Bits of offering food fly over his head. A metal bowl clatters on the courtyard. Shrieking "Yaaa! Yaaa!" the Chatterbox *Mansin* whirls the pig's legs around Grandfather Chon and pokes at his back with the hooves, then casts them away into the courtyard. She circles his head with a large kitchen knife. Sitting on his shoulders, she stabs at the air all around him. She holds the tip of the blade against his back. She rips the covering from his head. Reaching her arms round his body, she tears the yellow cloth. Now she offers him the bundle of five-colored divination flags. Grandfather Chon taps one of the sticks and the Chatterbox *Mansin* draws out Grandfather Chon's choice, a white flag indicating the benign influence of the Seven Stars, a significant deity in the Chon pantheon. "Alright!" she says; the exorcism is a success. They can stop here, no further pelting is necessary.

Now the Warrior spreads the pile of divination flags on the

floor, one on top of the other, and gestures for Grandfather Chon to cover the top flag with money. Grandmother Chon stands beside Grandfather Chon, handing him thousand-won bills to place on the flags. When the Warrior is satisfied with the money on one flag, he rolls it back to reveal another empty flag awaiting money. The Warrior is not easily satisfied and the daughter-in-law gets impatient. She tries to roll one of the flags back herself but is foiled by the Warrior who snaps the flag back in place. Finally satisfied, the Warrior hands Grandfather Chon an apple from the offering tray and sends him back to sleep in the inner room.

The Warrior Official (*Sinjang Taegam*) appears next, the greedy official serving under the martial spirits. The Warrior Official contemptuously flings away the pig's legs offerings, collects a few bills from the women, and sings a song of self praise. As she has begged all the deities, Grandmother Chon implores the Warrior Official to make her husband well and give her son success in business. This segment is brief. It is now three o'clock in the morning.

The women spread sleeping mats in the two hot floor rooms. Grandmother Chon and the *mansin* discuss the merits of various pharmacies in town before everyone falls asleep.

The next morning, everyone wakes up early. The women wash and cook the rice, and breakfast is over by nine. Some of the neighborhood women trail in to watch the completion of the *kut*. A few of the women ask the Chatterbox *Mansin* for advice. The Chatterbox *Mansin* approves of the direction of a comtemplated change in residence, cautions delay for a husband anxious to switch jobs, and gives instructions for a minor household ritual.

Meanwhile, Yongsu's Mother and the Town *Mansin* are having a quarrel. Yongsu's Mother complains that the Town *Mansin* merely drums and hits the cymbals without performing any of the segments, far more strenuous work. Yongsu's Mother insists that the Town *Mansin* perform the next segment for the House Lord in the roofbeam (*Songju*). The Town *Mansin* tries to beg off, "I haven't done a *kut* in three years, so I've forgotten what to say. Besides, my feet hurt."

"Lies!" shrieks Yongsu's Mother.

"But I don't have a Korean dress."

Yongsu's Mother throws a parcel at her. "Wear this, you'll

look so pretty." The Town *Mansin* performs the segment for the House Lord. Stirring a cup of wine with the tail of a dried fish offered to the House Lord, she flicks drops of wine up onto the roofbeam. She tosses up handfuls of rice grain from Grandfather Chon's bowl. She catches the rice in her hands, then counts the grains for an auspicious even number. The House Lord is pleased. The Town *Mansin* burns the paper announcement of the *kut* that the family had pasted to the roofbeam to inform the House Lord. The Chatterbox *Mansin* hastily balances the pig's legs on the battle fork while the Town *Mansin* sings final praises to the House Lord and removes her costume.

The Chatterbox *Mansin* urges the women to use the *mugam* again. Grandmother Chon dances first in the Great Spirit's yellow robe. As Grandmother Chon begins to dance, the Chatterbox *Mansin* hands her wine from the cups on the offering tray. Grandmother Chon rocks back and forth as the drum beats pick up speed. Grandmother Chon whirls on her feet, then picks up the pig's legs and runs into the inner room. She rubs her husband lightly with the pig's legs. There is soft chuckling from the women. Next, Grandmother Chon picks up the battle fork and sword and whirls with them. The shaman ancestress has ascended as Grandmother Chon's personal god.

The maternal aunt dances again. The paternal aunt dances next. Initially, Grandmother Chon's old friend dances beside the paternal aunt, singing a few bars of a popular song, "Goody, goody, cha, cha, cha." The paternal aunt starts jumping but soon stops.

"Why didn't you dance longer?" the women ask.

"I had a headache."

The Chatterbox *Mansin* tells her that she discerns the presence of an active Buddhist Sage in the paternal aunt's home and tells her to make special offerings to this spirit next year.

The Chatterbox *Mansin,* in a green robe, invokes the Mountebank (*Changbu*), the deity of dead actors and acrobats. While the Chatterbox *Mansin* sings the Mountebank's invocation, the maternal aunt begins to dance again. The Mountebank hits the maternal aunt with a fan and tweaks her breast. The Mountebank divines for Grandmother Chon, repeating the other gods' promises that things will improve. The Mountebank acknowledges the paternal aunt's numerous worries about health and finance and promises aid, but the paternal aunt must make the proper offerings. The Mountebank reassures the daughter and reminds her that she, too, has ritual responsibilities. She must honor the gods in her husband's home. Finally, the Mountebank tells the maternal aunt that she must change the date of her sixty-first birthday celebration to a more auspicious month and give feast food to the ancestors on the eve of the celebration (*yot'am*). Finally the Mountebank pulls the maternal aunt's clothing wide from her back and fans up good fortune. The maternal aunt beams.

The *kut* inside the house is finished. The Chatterbox *Mansin* presses her brass mirror into a tub of rice grain for a final prognosis of the house gods' pleasure. None of the grains stick. She tries with one of the cymbals. No luck. "Stupid prick!" she shouts, then claims that she can never perform this divination for her own regular clients. Yongsu's Mother presses the mirror into the rice. Four grains stick to the surface. She spills them in Grandmother Chon's skirt. The even number is the desired sign.

Moving Outside the House

The women of the family disassemble the offerings while Yongsu's Mother prepares to invoke the House Site Official (*T'oju Taegam*). With a swift invocation and dance on the porch, she puts on her shoes and runs to the back of the house, where a tub of rice cake on a tray awaits the House Site Official. "Wine!" snaps the Official, "Wine! Wine!" The daughter-in-law rushes up with a full kettle. The *Mansin* puts the tub of rice cake on her head and the House Site Official makes a progress through the courtyard and around the outer wall of the house, spilling cups of wine and throwing bits of rice cake. The daughter-in-law follows with the huge wine kettle, constantly filling the cup. The Official enters the courtyard and stands below the porch, demanding money from the daughter and daughter-in-law. The daughter says she has spent all her money, then slowly draws out another bill. The Official divines, predicting auspicious months and urging Grandmother Chon to seek medicine and acupuncture treatments for Grandfather Chon. The Official passes the tub of rice cake back to Grandmother Chon.

In the courtyard, Yongsu's Mother quickly invokes the Grain

God (*kollip*) who brings wealth into the house. She propitiates the Foundation God of the earth below the house (*Chisin*) with a libation of wine spilled in a circle in the front courtyard. Standing before the threshold, the *mansin* spills wine for the Door Guard (*Sumun Taegam*).

Back on the porch, the Chatterbox *Mansin* divides the money collected during the *kut*. Okkyong's Mother and the Town Mansin receive 12,000 won each. Yongsu's Mother receives 14,000 won for her more strenuous participation. The Chatterbox *Mansin* retains 18,000 won. She will also claim two thousand won from the final segment of the kut.[5] The *mansin* are very pleased with the amount of money taken in at this *kut*. The women spent freely. The maternal aunt was particularly generous. As usual, Yongsu's Mother feels that the Chatterbox *Mansin* took an excessively large share of the pay while she, Yongsu's Mother, performed the more exhausting Official's segments.

As the *mansin* in charge, the Chatterbox Mansin claims one of the pig's legs and all of the rice grain used to prop up her brass mirror during the *kut*. Each *mansin* takes home a generous package of rice cake and some candy and fruit from the offering tray. Grandmother Chon also gives rice cake to the women who helped her in the kitchen.

Everyone, including Grandfather Chon, moves outside the gate. The *mansin* bring out bundles of costumes, props, and rice cake. They set up a small tray of offering food. The Chatterbox *Mansin* again invokes the Soldier Official who appeared in the first segment. She is still singing the invocation when the daughter and daughter-in-law, carrying their bundles of rice cake, rush down the road to catch the bus for Seoul. Grandmother Chon begs the Soldier Official, "I'll make special offerings *(kosa)*. I'll give you another *kut* if you just help my son succeed in business." The Chatterbox *Mansin* invokes the *Sonang*, ancient scholars who died in literati purges or committed suicide over thwarted careers. Next come the restless ghosts, those who died violent or untimely deaths. The *mansin* chant them as they pass before her eyes: "Those who died of fevers, those who died on the road, those who died in traffic accidents, those who drowned, those who died in childbirth."

Finally, the Chatterbox *Mansin* beckons Grandfather Chon. He kneels facing the field with his back to the house. She piles another strip of yellow cloth and one of his own shirts on his head. Grandmother Chon brings a dead but unplucked chicken. The Chatterbox *Mansin* presses the chicken to Grandfather Chon's chest and rubs it against his back, then whirls it around his head and tosses it off into the fields. She pelts Grandfather Chon with millet. She dumps rice wine, vegetables and bits of candy from the offering tray into a gourd dipper and flings some of the food over Grandfather Chon's shoulders. She stabs at the air around Grandfather Chon's shoulders and head with a kitchen knife. She reaches around his chest and rips the thin yellow cloth, breaking the hold of wandering ghosts. Carrying the dipper full of scraps, she runs into the field and sets it down. Misfortune is lured away from the house.

The Chatterbox *Mansin* gives final instructions to Grandmother Chon. She must have someone bury the chicken on the hillside like a human corpse, and quickly burn the yellow cloth and the shirt from the exorcism.

The *mansin* politely decline Grandmother Chon's invitation to lunch and hasten down the road in the early afternoon sunshine to catch the bus.

Epilogue

The foregoing was not meant to be a proper folklorist's rendering of *kut*. One can find precise lists of deities, costumes, and offering food elsewhere.[6] I have presented one *kut* as I saw it, a living and loud event with some mistakes, much skill, clumsy moments, copious wine and considerable laughter.

There is flexibility in the structure of a *kut*. A basic list of spirits must be manifested in an appropriate order.[7] There is some variation in the way the main *mansin* chooses to structure a *kut*. The Chatterbox *Mansin* invoked the Birth Grandmother before the war gods in the Chon family *kut*. She could have switched the order. She combined the Buddhist Sage and the Seven Stars with the Birth Grandmother although the first two deities are most often invoked immediately before or immediately after the ancestors' segment.

The particular spiritual history of the Chon family appeared in the structure and drama of their *kut*. Ancestors vary from household to household: Is the grandmother still alive? Did the husband or wife have a prior spouse? Are there dead children or siblings? But there are also variations, from *kut* to *kut,* in the relative strength of various gods in the household pantheon. In the Chon family *kut,* the family's enduring obligation to the Great Spirit Grandmother was reflected in the deity's demands for a new robe. The Chons' Great Spirit Grandmother was particularly powerful because an ancestress of Grandmother Chon was a *mansin*. The dead *mansin* continued to exert influence on her descendants.

The Great Spirit Grandmother had an underling, a Great Spirit Official, who appeared in the Official's segment and echoed her demands for a new yellow robe. The *mansin* say, "There are ninety-nine Officials and you couldn't play them all in one day." There is some variation from house to house in the types of Officials appearing in the Official's segment but they are all greedy and humerous.

Grandfather Chon's mother made offerings to the Seven Stars, and prayed for the birth and health of her children. Women who marry into the Chon family have a ritual obligation to worship the Seven Stars. In households where women have no special debt to the Seven Stars, the *mansin* does not manifest this god beside the storage jars.

The Chon family *kut* was a healing rite *(uhwan kut)* in contrast to a *kut* for the family's prosperity and good fortune *(chaesu kut),* or a *kut* to send off the dead *(chinogi kut)*. Grandfather Chon and his illness claimed center stage at crucial moments in the *kut*. The *mansin* exorcised him twice and family women and neighbors importuned the spirits on his behalf.

Those familiar with the literature of healing rites will immediately recognize certain themes: the *kut* mustered group support — kin and neighbors — around the afflicted. The *mansin* with their drum, cymbals, and costumes, assaulted his senses with sound and color peaking in the percussive "shock therapy" of the two exorcisms. The *kut* was a dramatic "ritual process" aimed at transforming Grandfather Chon's orientation from "sick" to "cured." The transformation was most graphically symbolized in the final transference of Grandfather Chon's illness to the body of the white chicken that was buried like a corpse. (Kennedy 1973; Kiev et. al. 1964; Turner 1967, 1968; Torrey 1970).

As "ritual process," the *kut* is a long progression of segments spanning an evening, most of the night, and all of the following morning. One is struck, however, by Grandfather Chon's minimal participation in events performed ostensibly on his behalf. The *kut* was clearly a women's party. It was also a family ritual. While Grandmother Chon begged the gods and ancestors to make her husband well, she made equally emphatic pleas for her son's business success. She was also concerned with the fates of her grandchildren, securing the gods' and ancestors' promises to keep them safe and aid their studies. This was as it should be, for while the patient and his crisis claim center stage at various points in the *kut,* the total *kut* heals the entire family.

In the *mansin's* view, Grandfather Chon's illness was merely symptomatic of a greater malaise within the Chon family. The family's spiritual defenses had broken down. When the household gods are satisfied with offerings, they defend the integrity of the home against negative influences from without. When the gods haven't been given their due, they drop their guard. The dead move among the living. Wandering ghosts and noxious influences invade the house. Grandfather Chon's persistent illness revealed that the gods of the Chon family pantheon, most particularly the powerful Great Spirit Grandmother, were displeased. The *mansin* exorcised Grandfather Chon of wandering ghosts and noxious influences while the total process of the *kut* revitalized the Chon family's relationship with their household gods and ancestors. The son would prosper, the grandchildren flourish.

The house itself is the setting and prime metaphor of a *kut,* mediating between the family who reside within the rooms and the household gods the *mansin* manifest as they move through the dwelling. The process of a *kut* is a process through the house, from outside the gate, through the courtyard, onto the porch, into the inner room, around the inner court, and back outside the gate again. In the course of this pilgrimage, various gods appear to chastize, extort homage, and promise blessings, prosperity, health, and fertility.

Relationships between human and supernatural residents are patched up throughout the structure. The *mansin* pass tubs of rice cake, costumes, and pig's legs back to the family in the direction of the porch and hot floor rooms. The gods fan blessings into pockets and under clothing. They fill skirts with grain, nuts, and seeds. By holding a *kut*, the family catches positive influences and secures them within. The *mansin* cast pollutions, wandering ghosts, and noxious influences out beyond the gate. They confirm the expulsion of these negative forces with a cast of a knife, the tip of the blade pointing out, away from the open door.

Mansin use the term *kajong* to denote a *kut*-sponsoring group. In the purest sense, a *kajong* is a "home" or "household," those who dwell under one roof and share a budget. The Chon family *kajong* is Grandmother and Grandfather Chon. The son, his wife and their children form a separate *kajong* with their own residence, budget, and household pantheon. But the household pantheon of the son's family is colored and shaped by influences from the parents' home. The Great Spirit Grandmother and the Seven Stars, active in the parents' pantheon, are also active in the son's home. When the Chon daughter-in-law danced *mugam,* both the Great Spirit Grandmother and the Seven Stars rose up as her Body-governing Gods.

The fate of the son and his family is still connected to the fate of his parental home despite their separate residences. The son will eventually offer ancestor rites to his father and mother. The son's family is ultimately the continuation of the father's family. Supernatural malaise in the parents' house taints the fortunes of the son's family. The son's family benefits from blessings bestowed in the *kut* at the parents' home.

Women who have no legitimate claim to membership in the Chon *kajong* confronted the Chons' gods and received blessings at the *kut*. Korean society is patrilineal and patrilocal. Daughters marry out, relinquishing jural and ritual claims on their natal home, but they do not lose touch with their parents' gods. The Chon daughter returned for the *kut* and manifested the Great Spirit Grandmother, an influence from the Chon pantheon, when she danced *mugam*. Indeed, the daughter carried the Great Spirit Grandmother's influence with her to the pantheon of her affinal home just as Grandmother Chon, before her, carried the Great Spirit Grandmother's influence from her own natal home when she married into the Chon family.[8]

Other categories of non-Chon women were also represented at the *kut*. Grandmother Chon's own sister, the dancing maternal aunt, was an avid participant and generous financial contributor. Grandfather Chon's sister, another out-married Chon woman, came to the *kut,* danced in the *mugam,* and received divinations. Often at the center of the action, these women received blessings from the gods in proportion to their financial contributions.

Finally, by broadest extension, the benefits of *kut* reach neighbors and friends who contribute small amounts of cash to receive divinations, lucky wine, and sweets from the Birth Grand-mother's tray, to use the *mugam,* and simply enjoy the inebriated gaiety of a *kut.*

All of these women are not passive spectators, but a concerned chorus. They importune the deities and comment on the unfolding drama. They find almost everything funny if it doesn't make them weep. They approach the gods and ancestors much as they approach life, with a strong sharp tongue, a sense of humor, and a good cry.

Kut is the most elaborate dramatization of the Korean woman's ritual world. The assumptions of this world blur the clean line of a male-centered patrilineal and patrilocal society. What are the parameters of the Korean woman's ritual world? How does she move within it? Can she manipulate ancestors, ghosts, and deities to her own advantage? Is the *mansin* an ally? An exploration of Korean shamanism is ultimately a consideration of Korean women. The *mansin* is the prime ritual specialist and most articulate commentator on a vast matrix of woman-centered ritual and belief. The women bring to the *mansin* their tales of domestic strife, sickness, financial misfortune, money-making schemes, plans for the marriage of children, their life experience.

Appendix I

The Chon Family *Kut*

Segment	Gods Manifested	Place	*Mansin*
First Segment (*Haengju Mullin*)	Soldier Official (*Kunung Taegam*)	Outside the Gate	Chatterbox *Mansin*
Drum Song (*Pujong* = pollution)	expell and invoke	porch	"

Segment	Gods Manifested	Place	Mansin
Ancestors' Segment	distant dead (*sopsu*) Mountain God of Native Place (*Ponhyang Sansin*)	"	"
	Netherworldly Guard (*Kamang*)		
	Great Spirit Grand-mother (*Taesin Halmoni*)		
	ancestors (*chosang*)	porch and inner room	
Officials' Segment	Official (*Taegam*)	porch, circu-lates house site	Yongsu's Mother
	Great Spirit Official (*Taesin Taegam*)		
	Women use the *mugam*.		
Buddhist Sage's Segment	Buddhist Sage (*Pulsa*)	porch	Okkyong's Mother
	Seven Stars (*Ch'ilsong*)	storage jars	
	Birth Grandmother (*Chesok, Samsin Halmoni*)	inner room	
Segment	Gods Manifested	Place	Mansin
	Princess (*Hogu*)	porch	
	unredeemed souls (*chonang*)	"	
War Gods' Segment (*Sangori, Sangsan-gori*)	General (*Changgun*)	porch	Chatterbox Mansin
	Special Messenger (*Pyolsang = Pyolsong*)		
	Warrior (*Sinjang*)		
	Spirit Warrior Official (*Sinjang Taegam*)		
	Kut stops for the night.		

Segment	Gods Manifested	Place	Mansin
House Lord's Segment	House Lord (*Songju*)	porch	Town *Mansin*
	Women use the *mugam* again.		
Mountebank's Segment	Mountebank (*Changbu*)	porch	Chatterbox *Mansin*
Official of the House Site's Segment	House Site Official (*T'oju Taegam*)	rear of house to front courtyard	Yongsu's Mother
	Grain God (*Kollip*)		
	Foundation God (*Ch'isin*)		
	Door Guard (*Sumun Taegam*)	main gate	
Soldier Official's Segment	Soldier Official (*Kunung Taegam*)	outside the main gate	Chatterbox *Mansin*
Final Send-off (*Twitchon*)	ghosts invoked	outside the main gate	Chatterbox *Mansin*

The segments of the Chon family *kut* are standard building blocks, but the sequence varies slightly from *kut* to *kut*. Ch'oe and Chang (1967) list possible variations in the sequence of a *kut*. Their *mansin* informant lives near Enduring Pine Village. Kim T.G. (1978) gives yet another *kut* sequence performed by a *mansin* in Seoul. Yim (1970) diagrams variations by region and type of *kut*.

Notes

1. Figures from the 1964 *Korea Statistical Yearbook* and the 1976 *Seoul Statistical Yearbook* are courtesy of Barbara Young.
2. I have discussed *mugam* dancing in a short article with some attention to the religious and pscyhological implications of the dance. (Kendall 1977b).
3. *Chesok* literally means "Buddha Emperor" but the *mansin* and her clients explicitly equate *Chesok* with the Birth Spirit (*Samsin Halmoni*); thus, my gloss, "Birth Grandmother."
4. Sometimes identified as the "Smallpox God," but this attribute, like the disease, is happily no longer significant in rural Korea.

5. Grandmother Chon agreed to pay 40,000 won for the *kut*. She delivered the money in a bundle to the Chatterbox *Mansin* a few days before the *kut*. The Chatterbox *Mansin* returned the money to Grandmother Chon before the start of the *kut* and Grandmother Chon gave it back gradually in response to the gods' and ancestors' demands throughout the *kut*. The remainder of the money came from the other women—relatives, neighbors and friends—who bought wine, danced, and received divinations.

6. Ch'oe and Chang (1967) list major patterns and variations for *kut* in the area where I did my own research. The Ministry of Culture's cumulative volumes on the folk beliefs contain ample descriptive material on shaman ritual. Both of these works include recorded texts of shaman songs. T.G. Kim (1971) has also recorded texts.

7. See Appendix I.

8. Note that the son and daughter are children of Grandfather Chon's first wife, yet they inherit the spiritual influences Grandmother Chon brought to the Chon pantheon. Social, not biological, parenting is significant here.

Bibliography

Ch'oe Kil-Song and Chang Chu-Gun. *Kyonggido Chiyok Musok* (Shaman Practices of Kyonggi Province). Seoul: Ministry of Culture, 1967.

Kendall, Laurel. "Mugam: the Dance in Shaman's Clothing," *Korea Journal* 17 (12), 1977.

Kennedy, John G. "Cultural Psychiatry," Hongiman (ed.) *Handbook of Social and Cultural Anthropology*. Chicago: Rand McNally, 1973.

Kiev, Ari (ed.). *Magic, Faith, and Healing*. New York: Free Press, 1964.

Kim Tae-Gon. *Hanguk Muga Chip* vol. I. (Anthology of Korean Shaman Songs). Iri: Wongwang University Folklore Institute, 1971.

"Shamanism in the Seoul Area," *Korea Journal* 18 (6) pp. 39-51, 1978.

Ministry of Culture and Bureau of Cultural Properties Preservation. *Comprehensive Investigation of Korean Folk Belief (Hanguk Minsin Chonghap Chosa)*. Seoul: Ministry of Culture, Bureau of Cultural Properties Preservation, 1969.

Torrey, E.F. "Indigenous Psychotherapy: Theories and Techniques," *Current Psychiatric Therapies* 10, pp. 118-129, 1970.

Turner, Victor. *The Forest of Symbols: Aspects of Ndembu Ritual*. Ithaca: Cornell University, 1967.

The Drums of Affliction: A Study of Religious Process among the Ndembu of Zambia. Oxford: Clarendon, 1968.

Yim Sok-Jae. "*Hanguk Musok Yongu Sosol*" ("Introduction to Research on Korean Shamanism"), *Asea Yosong*. (In Korean; with English summary). 1970.

9 / Slave Rebellions in the Koryo Period, 936-1392

ELLEN SALEM

The history of slavery, though one of injustice, cruelty, and repression, is only infrequently punctuated by accounts of armed rebellion. Throughout classical antiquity there were only three slave revolts of note, all within a period from 135 to 75 B.C.[1] In the American South five hundred slaves, at the most, participated in the largest and one of the very few slave revolts—in Louisiana in 1811. Nat Turner's followers in Virginia numbered less than seventy-five, and participants in the three other revolts in the American South ranged from twenty-five to one hundred individuals.[2] The absence of revolts does not mean that slaves accepted their lot, although desire for liberation can hardly be said to be innate in the human race. Open insurrection was, however, dangerous and chances of success minimal. At the very best, a slave revolt was a calculated risk.[3]

Koryo stands apart. Between 1182 and 1232 the kingdom was beset by eight major slave rebellions.[4] Why? Was there something unique about the fifty years that prompted slaves to seek a radical solution?

To find an answer it is necessary first to examine the accounts of the rebellions contained in the few extant primary Koryo sources. If there is one unifying theme in the accounts, it is that slave rebellion was a symptom of bad rule; a theory that was invariably reduced to a human equation. In the more detailed accounts—some are very short—most attention was given to the personalities involved. When a proximate cause was ascribed to a rebellion, it was an individual's misdeed; most often, but not always, it was a slave's.

The accounts, taken individually, provide few clues to the reasons for a period of slave rebellions. Taken as a whole, they do. In the second section of this paper the rebellions are analyzed as a group. Of particular importance to this analysis is an understanding of the era in which the rebellion occurred. In brief, by the mid-twelfth century the growth of power of the civil officials had resulted in a loss of power, status and high ranking positions for the military officials. The situation came to a head in 1170 when Chong Chung-bu (1106-1179) massacred the civil officials at court and placed a new king on the throne. In 1179 Chong was killed by rivals and a fierce struggle for hegemony among various military contenders ensued. By 1196 Ch'oe Ch'ung-hon (1149-1219) had, by ruthlessly eliminating his rivals, achieved supremacy and by 1203 his rule was firmly established. The Ch'oe clan were the *de facto* rulers of the country until 1259. The period from 1170 to 1259 is commonly known as the Military Period. Theories formulated to explain the uncommon incidence of slave rebellions in the early years of the Military Period are discussed. Finally, the Koryo experience is examined in the light of slave rebellions in other, non-Asian societies.

The Koryo Slave Revolts

The Chonju Rebellion

The first of the slave rebellions under consideration began in Chonju in 1182. The official slaves in a government shipyard had for some time been laboring under a harsh official who was "resolutely extreme in the application of punishment." A call from the capital for additional ships prompted the slave Chuk-tong and six others to exhort their fellow slaves to rise in protest. Most did and they burned the home of Chin Tae-yu, the official responsible for enforcing the harsh corvee. When the rebels first met the government army, they charged that the new demands placed on them were not legal. The Royal Inspector took note of their complaints and "had no choice but to fetter Tae-yu and send him to the capital." The Royal Inspector then led an attack on the rebels, but they took refuge within the city wall where they were able to hold out for several months, thanks more to government mismanagement than rebel skill. Finally, the government troops succeeded in entering the city and killed about fifty slaves, apparently the total rebel force.

The immediate causes of this rebellion were clear—an overly harsh official and overly harsh demands. These slaves received a salary of sorts in exchange for a work or product quota.[5] Their charge of illegality suggests that they were not receiving a salary commensurate with an increased quota.

The Kil In Rebellion

Fourteen years later, in 1196, about one thousand slaves and eunuchs rallied to the call of General Kil In who rose in rebellion against Ch'oe Ch'ung-hon. The reason for the slaves' participation was not given. Was it the hope or promise of a reward or remission, or were there other factors, involved related to the Ch'oe assumption of power?

Kil In's attempt to overthrow the Ch'oes was summarily squashed and all the rebels killed by a superior military force. The histories place no weight on the slaves' participation and treat the uprising as one caused by the political aspirations of one man.[6]

The Manjok Rebellion

The Manjok rebellion is the stuff of sweeping theories and persistent mythology about the innate aspirations of the downtrodden. In 1198, in Kaegyong, the house slave Manjok and six others assembled a group of public and private slaves with a mind to persuading them to rebel. The leaders argued that since the military coup of 1170 many former slaves had become generals and ministers. Should not they, too, who suffered under the sharpness of the whip, throw off the fetters that bound them to their fate? The assembled agreed and made plans to gather several days later on the polo field. After killing Ch'oe Ch'ung-hon each would kill his master and burn the slave registers.[7]

At the initail meeting Manjok voiced his hope that the eunuchs and palace slaves would, on seeing a large crowd of rebellions slaves, lend their support to the rebels and "cull out the bad ones within" the palace and take possession of the government centers.[8]

The day of the uprising saw only a few hundred slaves at the polo field and the uprising was postponed, never to occur. A private slave told his master of Manjok's plot and the master informed Ch'oe Ch'ung-hon who promptly seized Manjok and one hundred of his cohorts and had them drowned. The remaining conspirators were not sentenced; the informer was remitted and given a reward of eighty ounces of silver.[9]

The Chinju Rebellion

The fourth of Koryo's major slave uprisings began in Chinju, Kyongsang Province, in 1200. In the account of this uprising the slaves were not center stage. Rather, their rebellion provided the backdrop for the tale of a scoundrel, Chong Pang-ui.

Chong was one of fifty local officials whose residences were burned by a group of public and private slaves in 1200. Furious, Chong demanded that the local magistrate, Yi Sun-jung, give him sole authority to seek out and punish the slaves. The magistrate, suspicious of Chong, branded him a rebel and had him cast into jail. Two days later Chong's brother, Ch'ang, rushed the jail and released him. Together, the brothers pillaged the countryside and were said to have killed 6,400 individuals. When a royal commissioner came to investigate, the district officials, terrified of Chong, laid the blame for the local upset on Yi Sun-jung, who was summarily banished. A second inspection team was sent from the captial and though soon aware of Chong's activities, they "merely looked on with arms folded."

At that time, two bandit leaders were competing with Chong in laying waste the countryside. Twenty or so inhabitants of Chinju, presumably slaves, sought refuge with the two bandit groups, based in the *ch'onmin pugok* of Nool, and together they attacked Chong.[10] The combined forces were easily routed and Chong wiped out the insurgents from Nool. In the following year the people of Chinju killed Chong. His brother led two hundred troops to take the city but was defeated. "With that, Chinju was pacified."[11]

The Milsong Rebellion

Also in the year 1200 about fifty government slaves in Milsong (present-day Miryang), Kyongsang Province, seized the weapons in the government armory and joined the Unmun bandit group. Nothing further is recorded about these slaves, but presumably they were readily accepted by the bandits. Five months after the Milsong slaves joined the bandit group, monks from Puin and Tonghwa temples also threw in their lot with the bandits, and for several years the group succeeded in harassing the government.[12] Clearly, the slaves were not alone in their protests against existing conditions. The eight major slave revolts that occurred between 1182 and 1232 were more than matched by eight peasant revolts between 1199 and 1217, but only rarely did the two combine forces.

The Woodgatherers' Rebellion

In 1203 a sizeable group of house slaves, who customarily worked on the outskirts of the capital gathering firewood, took advantage of their opportunities to congregate and formed military training companies. Their threatening posture soon came to the attention of Ch'oe Chung-hon, and he dispatched troops to seize them. Forewarned, they all fled, but fifty were caught, questioned under torture, and then tossed into the river.[13] Who organized these slaves? What were their aims? The sources are silent.

The Revolt of the Slave Troops of Ch'ungju

After that abortive attempt toward an unknown goal in 1203, Koryo's slave population was quiescent for nearly thirty years until 1231 when two insurrections occurred, both occasioned by the Mongol Invasions of Korea.

The revolt of the slaves in Ch'ungju in the first month of 1232 was the result of a miscarriage of justice. In the previous year, when the Mongol troops were nearing Ch'ungju, two defense forces—one gentry and one slave—were formed. The forces were led by two men who had long been enemies. When the Mongol troops approached Ch'ungju, the gentry patrol fled, and so did the commander of the slave army. A monk, Ubon, and Chi Kwang-su, a low ranking military officer, filled the void and led the remaining slave troops in a rout of the invaders.

The victorious slaves were not hailed as saviors of the city. When the officials and soldiers returned, many of them, including the leader of the gentry patrol, accused the slaves of plundering public and private treasures. Even worse, the township headman, Kwang Ip, and five cohorts plotted in secret to kill the leaders of the slave army. The slaves, already incensed by the accusations made against them, could stand no more. Using a hoax burial as a pretext, they assembled and decided to slaughter rather then be slaughtered. First they murdered the chief conspirators against their leaders and then sought out and killed those against whom they bore grudges. The number killed is not known, but the sources note that even the wives and children of those the slaves considered enemies were not spared.[14]

Aid was requested from the capital and two officials were promptly dispatched to Ch'ungju. Upon arrival they did not immediately move against the slaves; rather, one of them brought Chi Kwang-su and Ubon to the capital where they were taken before the military ruler, Ch'oe Yi.[15] Ch'oe generously rewarded the two as leaders of the rout of the Mongols, but his conciliatory act came too late.[16] The slaves holding the city would not surrender and Ubon returned to Ch'ungju and resumed his position as their leader. The rebels were able to hold the city for seven months because the government could not spare troops to move against them, but in the eighth month of 1232 a sizeable force led by Yi Cha-song was dispatched.[17] Yi's prompt defeat of the slaves owed more to treachery from within the stronghold than attack from without. Several of the leaders of the slave army met with Yi and offered to decapitate the ringleaders and then force a surrender. Yi agreed to their terms, promising not to slay those who surrendered.

The traitorous slaves returned within the walls of the city and killed Ubon, whereupon many of the slaves fled the city. Yi waited two days, entered the city, captured the remnants of the band, and killed them all. The booty was brought to the capital as tribute.[18]

The Kaegyong Rebellion

Yi Cha-song's victory over the rebels in Ch'ungju followed close upon his victory over rebellious slaves in Kaegyong in the seventh month of 1232. In that month the king deserted his capital on the mainland for the island refuge, Kanghwa. The move was attended by great suffering:

> At that time the rains continued for ten days. Sinking up to their knees in mire, men and horses fell prostrate. Of those who reached the official headquarters there were even wives of good families who had come barefoot, carrying burdens on their heads. One could not bear to hear the widowers and widows, orphaned and childless, crying for those they had lost.[19]

The misery of those who remained, though not recorded, must have been equally severe. Fear and hunger must have been the lot of many. In the all but deserted capital a government slave runner named Yi T'ong organized the commoners and monk-laborers in Kyonggi Province and the slaves who had been left in the capital. Together they drove out the officials of the token government left in Kaegyong, removed documents related to their status from the government offices, and plundered public and private granaries. The government soon heard of this and sent three armies to punish the rebels. The two forces met in battle some miles from Kaegyong and the rebel army was defeated.

An insurgent group of slaves, peasants, and monks still held Kaegyong. A government Night Patrol tricked the gate guards into believing that they were members of the rebel army, fresh from victory over the government forces. The guards opened the gates and the patrol entered, decapitated the guards, and killed the leader of the revolt, the slave Yi T'ong. Government success was then a matter of course, and the rebels were wiped out.[20]

As with all the slave revolts recorded in the histories, information is meager. Several features, however, seem to set this revolt apart from the others. It was the only recorded instance of slaves plundering granaries. It was also the sole recorded instance of large-scale commoner participation in what was essentially a slave revolt.

One need not look far for the causes of this seeming anomaly—hunger and generalized hysteria. Yi T'ong's rallying cry may well have been food, not freedom. The Mongols had laid waste the countryside. The commoners had suffered and would suffer more. The rich, powerful, and well connected could abandon their homes for an island refuge leaving slaves and "good" farmers behind to face the enemy and supply the food for those who had fled. Small wonder that a government slave could rally a diverse band—all oppressed and all exploited.[21]

Causes of the Rebellions

A number of theories have been advanced to explain the uncommon incidence of slave revolts during the Military Period. They range from the simple or conventional to the complex and innovative.

Some see slave revolts and commoner revolts as the same phenomenon. Long pressed beyond endurance, commoner and slave rose against the government in protest of their lot as soon as opportunity presented itself.[22] Others place more weight on the desire of the slaves to escape the strictures of their status, but do not dismiss economic deprivation as a factor.[23] Still others attribute the slave revolts to a wider combination of causes including the relaxation of official discipline, acquisition of official posts by slaves, rampant violence, and the harsh treatment of slaves.[24]

Pyon T'ae-sop, who has studied Koryo slave rebellions, believes that their causes can be found in an analysis of the slave system in and of itself. Slave rebellions and commoner rebellions must be regarded as separate phenomena springing from different sources; economic factors can also be excluded as a motivating force in the slave rebellions. Rather, under the early rule of the military, a number of slaves rose in status; the success of some led to rising expectations which, however, were inevitably frustrated, prompting the slaves to rebel.[25]

Diametrically opposed to this thesis is one proposed by Schultz. He believes that a number of slaves were able to improve their status prior to the military takeover. When the Ch'oes came into power they were intent upon tightening the social order which, in effect, brought a halt to remissions. The slaves then revolted in reaction to the Ch'oes' stringent social policies.[26]

Sufficient evidence does not exist to adopt or dismiss any theory with complete certainty. Least satisfactory are those theories which stress economic deprivation. World history has shown that hunger and hardship alone have seldom been the decisive factors in rebellions. If anything, slave and peasant rebellions tend to be preceded by a perceptible improvement in the lot of the downtrodden. In Koryo, the growth of the great estates provided opportunities for economic advancement for some slaves, though not for the commoners. Most telling, however, is the fact that in only one of the revolts were granaries raided.

Heightened social consciousness cannot be dismissed as an important contributing factor to the unrest of the times. Remission either granted or curtailed does not, however, provide the key to the sudden activation of the slaves' desire to throw off their shackles.

Uijong's reign (1146-1170), which preceded the military

takeover, was not marked by an unusual number of remissions. But the fact that Uijong's favorite was a slave prompted many contemporaries and later commentators to see an untoward advance for all slaves at this time. Paucity of remissions also marked the Military Period although the confusion of the times, particularly in the early years, did facilitate extra-legal status change for some. That period, too, saw several men of slave ancestry reach positions of prominence—though certainly not to the extent that was seen in the Mongol period. Both during the Military Period, and in the years directly prior to it, it was not uncommon for slaves to act as agents for their masters in their drive to acquire land and slaves. While the slave-agents were not remitted, the power invested in them did affect a status change.

In the generalized social instability of the Military Period the slaves saw the potential for change. It was readily apparent to them that the social structure had, at the very least, been shaken. Might not the fissures that had provided opportunity for some provide opportunity for the slave as well?

Departures from the strict social norm were not unique to the Military Period. They were far more pronounced during the period of Mongol overlordship, yet while the Mongols actually held power, slave revolts ceased.

No one factor can be singled out as the cause of the slave revolts. During the Military Period a number of conditions existed which made slave revolts feasible. In a study of slave revolts in the Americas—one of the few of true comparative scope—Genovese has identified a number of elements which, existing simultanously, tended to be present when slave revolts occurred in the Western hemisphere. They were: (1) a master-slave relationship that developed more as a matter of business than as a paternal relationship, (2) economic distress and unusual hardship that prevailed with greater frequency than in the American South, (3) large slaveholding units, (4) urban centers and great plantation districts that offered especially favorable conditions, (5) a high ratio of slave to free, (6) slaves with military experience, and (7) a division of the ruling class.[27]

With slight modifications, all of these features were present during the Military Period.

It cannot be denied that paternalism marked many a master-slave relation; indeed, paternalism may be said to have characterized Koryo society in general. But the impact of paternalism, the mutual bonds of loyalty and responsibility were, for the slaves who lived apart from their masters, for the absentee slaves and for public slaves working in large-scale enterprises, considerably weakened if they existed at all. Contact between an absentee slave and his master was often limited to his yearly payment of half his crop to the master or his agent—surely an act that did not foster love, loyalty, or dependence. Some private slaves were jointly owned, others were rented out by their masters—again, conditions that made the master-slave relationship one of business.

Of the eight revolts during the Military Period, private slaves were the sole participants in only one—the woodgatherers' revolt in 1203. Public and private slaves joined together in three uprisings: Manjok's in 1198, Chinju in 1200, and Kaegyong in 1271. The participants in the other four—Chonju in 1182, Kil In in 1196, Milsong in 1200, and the Ch'ungju slave troops in 1232—were public slaves. Moreover, the large slave population of mid-Koryo and the changing patterns of land-tenancy necessitated the deployment of most private slaves in a business-like manner, working their masters' fields often as absentee slaves.

Be that as it may, the propensity to revolt does not depend on the presence or absence of paternalism, though it must be taken into account. It is worth noting that in the American War between the States slave owners were often hurt and bewildered when "old Jim, my faithful butler for twenty years" went off and joined the Union forces as soon as he had the chance.[28]

Economic distress was clearly the decisive factor in only one revolt, that of the Kaegyong slaves, Kyonggi commoners, and monk-laborers in 1271. It is possible that the fifty officials whose homes were set on fire by the Chinju slaves had been extorting grain from the slaves in the locality—most of whom may well have been absentee slaves.

Two other revolts, in Chonju in 1182 and in Ch'ungju in 1232, were responses to specific injustices—starvation not among them; nor was hunger mentioned in Manjok's speech. It is possible that the economic ills of the times had visited themselves on the slaves' diet and this made the slaves who joined both Manjok and Kil In more amenable to revolt—but this is only conjecture. Most historians, however, feel that the slave in mid-Koryo was better fed than the commoner. The economic well-being of the Koryo slave was in no way comparable to his peers in the American South, however. In 1860 the American slave consumed 4,185 calories a day, a figure not matched in most of the world today, and certainly not by the majority of medieval Koreans, whether slave or non-slave.[29]

In sum, with the exception of the Kaegyong revolt, economic deprivation must be dismissed as a prime factor in inciting slaves to revolt. Here, however, the word "prime" is emphasized. The breakdown of the land system that began in Myongjong's reign (1170-1197) brought with it generalized economic instability and hunger for many. It stands to reason that in a malfunctioning economy some slaves, particularly absentee slaves, as well as the majority of commoner farmers would be affected.

While the effects of the breakdown of the land system on the size of the slaves' rice bowls is problematical, its effects on the size of the slave population are not. From Uijong's reign on, there was a very substantial increase in the number enslaved. Most of this increased must have occurred in Kyonggi and Cholla provinces where most of the large estates were located and coincidentally the places where many of the slave revolts occurred. It is clear from the accounts of the rebellions that cities and prime agricultural areas were the sites of Koryo's slave revolts.

It is an understatement to say that the period of consolidation of Ch'oe rule was one of division of the ruling classes. Armed rebellions, plots, and counterplots were commonplace. Almost as soon as the turmoil of the early years of Ch'oe rule subsided, the country was faced with the Mongol invasions, and again divisiveness existed in the ruling class.

The most decisive condition affecting the feasiblity of slave revolt was that both the military takeover and the Mongol invasions gave the slaves ample opportunity to gain military experience. Many slaves participated in the infighting that accompanied the Ch'oe takeover, and many more were recruited to fight the Mongols. Moreover, the generally belligerent character of the fifty years under consideration would assure that even slaves who had not joined in battle would not be unfamiliar with military practices and were psychologically conditioned to see violence as the method of problem-solving. Violence does breed violence. If one factor is to be singled out as the most important of the pre-conditions for the slave revolts it is that.

Notes

Abbreviations:

KS   Chong In-ji et. al. *Koryosa*. Seoul: Tongbanghak Yon'guso, 1955. First published 1454.

KSC   Kim Chong-so et. al. *Koryosa choryo*. Seoul: Tonggukmunhwasa, 1960. First published 1453.

1. Robin Winks, ed., *Slavery: A Comparative Perspective* (New York: New York University Press, 1972), p. 12.

2. Eugene D. Genovese, *Roll, Jordan, Roll* (New York: Pantheon Books, 1974), pp. 592-93.

3. Carl N. Degler, *Neither Black Nor White* (New York: Macmillan Co., 1971), pp. 50-51.

4. Pyon T'ae-sop includes the revolt of the *so* in Kongju in his study of Koryo slave revolts. Pyon T'ae-sop, "Manjok nan p'alsaeng ui sahoejok saji," *Sahak yon'gu*, vol. 4 (July 1959), pp. 1-43, esp. p. 28. No mention of slave participation occurs, however, in the three entries on that uprising and thus it is outside the scope of the study. KS 19:19:28b5 and KS 19:19:29b5 and KS 56:10:27a2. Also, the insubordination of three slaves during Uijong's reign was a fabrication and is therefore not considered in this chapter. KS 90:3:29.

5. The *Koryosa* mentions that a salary was given to artisans. KS 80:34:lb. For specific amounts see KS 80:34:30a-35b. Cho Ki-jun writes that in Silla the government's needs were supplied mainly by agricultural slaves who produced, as part of their corvee, various hand-crafted items. By Koryo, however, individuals were available who specialized in one field, no longer working as part-time farmer and part-time craftsman. The government then singled out certain government slaves and assigned them the corvee of providing specific items for government and court use and paid them a stipend in exchange for their services. Cho Ki-jun, *Choson kyongjesa* (Seoul: Ilsinsa, 1962), pp. 146-147. For the account of the rebellion see KSC 12:49:2a-6b.

6. KSC 13:35a-36a and KS 129:42:2b5-4a4.

7. KS 129:42:12a.

8. KSC 14:2a.

9. KS 129:42:12a.

10. The identity of both the twenty men who joined the bandit group at Nool and the defenders in the final seige of Chinju is questionable. In both instances the character used for the participants is 人 one not usually employed when referring to slaves. Pyon T'ae-sop, who has studied those rebellions, however, accepts without explanation the slave status of both groups. Nonetheless, the existence of negative evidence only places this rebellion in a problematical category. Pyon T'ae-sop, p. 35.

11. KS 128:41:25b-26b and KSC 14:6a-b.

12. KS 12:21:11a and KS 21:21:14a7 and KSC 14:6b.

13. KSC 14:12b and KS 129:42:15b7-9.

14. KSC 16:10a6-b9.

15. KS 23:23:10a.

16. KS 129:42:37a8-b2.

17. KSC 16:15b2-3.

18. KSC 16:16, 1-6.

19. KSC 16:14b10-15a2.

20. KSC 16:14b10-15b2 and KS 103:16:37a2-b4.

21. The last slave revolt that occurred in the period of Ch'oe control, that of 1271, has little in common with the revolts that preceded it. Though led by two slaves, its character and goals were at one with the aims of the Revolt of the Three Patrols—to continue to fight the Mongols and overthrow those who sought peace or even accommodation. In brief, two public slaves, Sunggyom and Kongdok organized a plot to kill the Mongol and pro-Yuan Koryo administrators in Kaegyong and then join with the Three Patrol forces on the island of Chin in the south-west. Their plans were discovered, revealed to the king, and the plotters executed. KS 27:27:5a8 and KS 27:28:9a9 and KS 123:36:13a8 and KS 13:36:13b9 and KS 30:43:9b. Such an action cannot be considered a slave revolt but it does indicate that even slaves considered themselves an integral part of the country and society that enslaved them. Koryo's final slave revolt occurred ten years before the fall of the dynasty. Three private slaves in Hapchu in Kyongsang Province proclaimed themselves generals, assembled followers, and "plundered in swarms." They planned to kill their masters and the magistrate but were apprehended and killed. KSC 31:31b1-4 and KS 134:47:35b3-6. The number of slaves involved in this revolt is not stated. It was more than a handful, but the brevity of the notices and the apparent ease with which the rebels were captured indicates that it was a localized uprising of several dozen slaves at the most.

22. Takashi Hatada, *A History of Korea* (Santa Barbara: Clio Press, 1969), pp. 47-48; Han Woo-keun, *The History of Korea* (Seoul: Eul-yoo Publishing Co., 1970), pp. 159-164.

23. Yi Ki-baek, *Han'guksa sillon* (Seoul: T'aesongsa, 1961), pp. 167-170.

24. Keizo Kameda, "Korai no dohi ni tsuite," *Seikyu Gakuso*, no. 16 (1936), pp. 63-70.

25. Pyon T'ae-sop, pp. 1-3, 37-41.

26. Edward Schultz, *The Ch'oe Military Dictatorship*, Ph.D. dissertation, University of Hawaii (1976), pp. 249-256.

27. Genovese, *Roll, Jordan, Roll*, pp. 590-591. A final item: "religions or syncretisms capable of calling slaves to holy war" does not apply in Korea because of the racial and homogeneity of master and slave. The slaves had no alien gods to call on who could strike terror into the hearts of their enemies.

28. Genovese, *Roll, Jordan, Roll*, pp. 97-112.

29. Robert William Fogel and Stanley L. Engerman, *Time on the Cross*, Vol. 1 (Boston: Little, Brown & Co., 1974), p. 112.